Mastering Veeam Backup & Replication

Design and deploy a secure and resilient Veeam 12 platform using best practices

Chris Childerhose

BIRMINGHAM—MUMBAI

Mastering Veeam Backup & Replication

Copyright © 2023 Packt Publishing

Associate Group Product Manager: Mohd Riyan Khan
Associate Publishing Product Manager: Khushboo Samkaria
Senior Editors: Nihar Kapadia and Divya Vijayan
Technical Editor: Nithik Cheruvakodan
Copy Editor: Safis Editing
Project Coordinator: Aryaa Joshi
Proofreader: Safis Editing
Indexer: Subalakshmi Govindhan
Production Designer: Jyoti Chauhan
Marketing Coordinator: Marylou De Mello

First published: February 2021
Second edition: February 2022
Third edition: April 2023

Production reference: 1250423

Published by Packt Publishing Ltd.
Livery Place
35 Livery Street
Birmingham
B3 2PB, UK.

ISBN 978-1-83763-009-7

www.packtpub.com

To all my colleagues and fellow Vanguards, who spoke words of encouragement and praise about my writing a book. It is truly humbling to have a great community in the Veeam Vanguards/Legends and colleagues that support your work.

– Chris Childerhose

Contributors

About the author

Chris Childerhose is an information technology professional with 27+ years of experience in network/systems architecture and design, network and systems administration, and technical support. He is a Veeam Vanguard/Legend and is a Veeam Certified Architect and Veeam Certified Engineer. He also has the following certifications: vExpert, Tanzu Vanguard, AWS Community Builder, VCAP-DCA, VCP-DCV, and MCITP. He currently works for ThinkOn as the lead infrastructure architect, where he designs the infrastructure for all client services offered. Chris is also an avid blogger on all things virtual, focusing on Veeam and Vmware, and is also the author of the first and second editions of *Mastering Veeam Backup & Replication*.

Writing a book is challenging and more rewarding than I could have ever imagined, but a third book is still quite a task. None of this would have been possible without my wife, Julie. She stood by me during every struggle and all my successes, including many nights of writing. She was someone I could talk to about my book and how things were going. She always pushes me, and I will be forever thankful for this.

I'm eternally grateful to Matt Crape and Rick Vanover from Veeam, who took the time to do a technical review of my third book and all of my chapters when they didn't have to. They were great at suggesting changes or edits and even contributed to chapters where necessary. I genuinely have no words to thank them for this amazing selflessness to help a fellow Veeamer on a third book about Veeam.

About the reviewer

Craig Dalrymple is a Scottish solutions architect at 11:11 Systems and is the co-leader/founder of the UK Veeam User Group. He has 25+ years of experience within the IT industry.

Table of Contents

Preface   xi

Part 1: Installation – Best Practices, Core Architecture, and Other Enhancements

1

Installation – Best Practices and Optimizations   3

Technical requirements	3	Understanding the Scale-Out Backup Repository	24
Understanding the best practices and optimizations for Veeam installation	4	VeeaMover	33
Installing Veeam Backup & Replication v12	4	SOBR Rebalance	33
Configuring and optimizing Proxy Servers	17	Upgrading Veeam Backup & Replication to v12	34
How to set up Repository Servers for success	21	Summary	44
		Further reading	45

2

Core Architecture Enhancements   47

Technical requirements	47	Learning about the Linux hardened repository option in the repository wizard	54
Introducing a PostgreSQL server for your database	48		
Understanding per-VM backup changes	51	Exploring new Linux proxy roles	57
		Summary	60
		Further reading	61

3

Scale-Out Backup Repository – What's New   63

Technical requirements	63	Using SOBR Rebalance and exporting data	72
Understanding sending backup data direct to Object Storage with SOBR	64	Exporting backups	76
Exploring VeeaMover and its benefits	66	Summary	81
Use cases for VeeaMover	66	Further reading	81

4

Tape Servers and Other Enhancements   83

Technical requirements	83	NAS backup to tape and improved LTO9 support	96
Understanding what is new with tape servers and object storage to tape	84	Other enhancements – permissions, exporting, and exclusions	98
Using Linux for a tape server	84	Summary	104
Object storage to tape	90	Further reading	104

Part 2: Security, Object Storage Direct, CDP, and Cloud Connect

5

Veeam's New Enhanced Security Features   107

Technical requirements	107	Understanding Linux – SSH or SUDO are not required	117
Understanding MFA and gMSA support	108	Discovering the new Auto-Logoff feature	117
Additional MFA settings	112	Summary	120
Benefits of using gMSAs	113	Further reading	120

6

Object Storage – What's New and Enhancements   121

Technical requirements	121	Configuring a backup copy job with GFS retention to immutable object storage	133
Understanding new direct-to-object storage and its use in SOBR	122	Discovering third-party integrations within the console for Azure and Wasabi	139
A standard repository backup job	131	Wasabi Object storage	140
SOBR backup job	132	Microsoft Azure Storage	141
Understanding GFS backups to object storage with immutability	132	Summary	142
		Further reading	142

7

What's New in NAS Backup   143

Technical requirements	143	Learning about health check features and the cloud helper appliance	162
Understanding NAS backup – archive copy mode and direct-to-object storage	144	The health check utility	163
		The cloud helper appliance	165
Understanding NAS backup with immutability support	152	Summary	171
Discovering NFS backup publishing as an SMB share	155	Further reading	172

8

CDP and Veeam Cloud Connect   173

Technical requirements	173	Investigating Instant VM Recovery within Veeam Cloud Connect	194
Discovering CDP to vCD in Veeam Cloud Connect	173	Summary	203
Exploring CDP with vCD to vCD	186	Further reading	204

Index   205

Other Books You May Enjoy   212

Preface

Veeam is one of the leading modern data protection solutions, and learning about this technology can help you protect your virtual environments effectively. This book guides you through implementing modern data protection solutions for your cloud and virtual infrastructure with Veeam. You will even gain in-depth knowledge of advanced-level concepts such as **Continuous Data Protection** (**CDP**) with Veeam Cloud Connect, Direct to Object storage, Instant Recovery, SOBR Rebalance, VeeaMover, and many core architecture changes.

Who this book is for

You will be a VMware administrator or backup administrator with some existing knowledge of Veeam and the topics covered in this book. You will know about some virtualization and backup concepts to understand what gets discussed in each chapter. Veeam is one of the leading modern data protection solutions, and learning about this technology will help you protect your environment. You might want to implement many of the topics discussed and possibly look into cloud providers to use Veeam Cloud Connect services.

What this book covers

Chapter 1, Installation – Best Practices and Optimizations, covers the upgrade and installation for Veeam Backup & Replication v12. You will learn how to set up things such as the backup server, proxies, repositories, and more. There will be a reference to the **Veeam Best Practices** site as well. Once installation and upgrade are covered, we will dive further into adding things such as repository servers, proxy servers, and more.

Chapter 2, Core Architecture Enhancements, covers many of the new core enhancements in the Veeam Backup & Replication v12 software. You will learn about the new database option to replace SQL Server: PostgreSQL. We will also look at the new per-VM backup chains, which will make management simpler and easier for troubleshooting. Finally, we will look at some new Linux features, such as a specific selection option for hardened repository and using Linux as a proxy.

Chapter 3, Scale-Out Backup Repository – What's New, covers the **scale-out backup repository (SOBR)** and what Veeam has added to make management easier. You can go directly to object storage now as well as have multiple buckets per SOBR tier. We will also look at VeeaMover, a new technology that allows you to move backups within a SOBR extent to another extent or even a new SOBR. We will also look at VeeaMover to move VMs between jobs, and jobs between repositories. Lastly, we will look at the new Rebalance option for the SOBR, which helps manage capacity between the extents as well as exporting from a SOBR in the Capacity or Archive tiers.

Chapter 4, Tape Server and Other Enhancements, covers the tape server and other enhancements within Veeam Backup & Replication v12. You will be shown how you can now have the tape server role on Linux as well as how sending from object storage to tape is now an option. We will look at NAS backup to tape, as well as better LTO9 support. Lastly, we will take a look at other changes such as restoring "Permissions Only" for files, exporting VM disks to another Hypervisor, and VM exclusions, which now include excluding them from jobs.

Chapter 5, Veeam's New Enhanced Security Features, discusses all things security-related within Veeam Backup & Replication v12. We will first look at the new MFA option within the console and support for gMSA security groups. We next look at how there will no longer be a need for SSH or SUDO within a Linux server. Lastly, we will take a look at the Auto Logoff feature within the console, allowing backup administrators to keep resources low.

Chapter 6, Object Storage – What's New and Enhancements, discusses what is new within object storage as well as enhancements within Veeam Backup & Replication v12. We will first look at the *Direct to Object* option, which everyone has been waiting for, including adding object storage to the Performance tier of a SOBR. We next look at how immutability can be turned on for GFS backups. Lastly, we will take a look at how third-party integrations have changed for things such as Azure Cool tier and Blob immutability, along with the new Wasabi integration wizard.

Chapter 7, What's New in NAS Backup, discusses what is new within NAS backup for Veeam Backup & Replication v12. We will first look at the new Archive Copy Mode and NAS backup to object storage as a target. We next look at how NAS backup supports immutability now. We will take a look at how you can publish an NFS as an SMB share for restore. Lastly, we will take a look at the improved health check and Cloud Helper appliance.

Chapter 8, CDP and Veeam Cloud Connect, discusses enhancements to CDP and Veeam Cloud Connect within Veeam Backup & Replication v12. We will first look at how customers can use CDP for **vCD (Cloud Director)** within a Cloud Connect environment. We next look at how you can use CDP to go from vCD to vCD. Lastly, we will take a look at how service providers can do an instant VM recovery within the Veeam Cloud Connect console using the backups on the repository servers.

To get the most out of this book

You should have at least 6 months of hands-on knowledge with Windows/Linux servers and virtualization with VMware, and it would be best if you were comfortable setting up servers and configuring them with storage. You should also have some backup knowledge and have already used Veeam, even for basic tasks, since many topics in the book look at the more advanced features of Veeam Backup & Replication.

Software/hardware covered in the book	Operating system requirements
Windows 2019/2022	Windows
Veeam Availability Suite	Windows
Ubuntu Linux 20.04 – Hardened Repositories	Linux

You need to have Windows Server set up to install Veeam Backup & Replication. You'll also need to have the Veeam Availability Suite ISO file and trial license downloaded from `http://www.veeam.com`.

Download the color images

We also provide a PDF file that has color images of the screenshots and diagrams used in this book. You can download it here: `https://packt.link/ep03i`.

Conventions used

There are a number of text conventions used throughout this book.

`Code in text`: Indicates code words in text, database table names, folder names, filenames, file extensions, pathnames, dummy URLs, user input, and Twitter handles. Here is an example: "Run the `setup.exe` file on the mounted ISO drive"

Bold: Indicates a new term, an important word, or words that you see onscreen. For instance, words in menus or dialog boxes appear in **bold**. Here is an example: "Before installing **Veeam Backup & Replication v12**, you must ensure that you have a server deployed, based on the Technical requirements in the preceding section, with enough disk space for the installation."

> **Tips or important notes**
> Appear like this.

Get in touch

Feedback from our readers is always welcome.

General feedback: If you have questions about any aspect of this book, email us at customercare@ packtpub.com and mention the book title in the subject of your message.

Errata: Although we have taken every care to ensure the accuracy of our content, mistakes do happen. If you have found a mistake in this book, we would be grateful if you would report this to us. Please visit www.packtpub.com/support/errata and fill in the form.

Piracy: If you come across any illegal copies of our works in any form on the internet, we would be grateful if you would provide us with the location address or website name. Please contact us at copyright@packt.com with a link to the material.

If you are interested in becoming an author: If there is a topic that you have expertise in and you are interested in either writing or contributing to a book, please visit authors.packtpub.com.

Share Your Thoughts

Once you've read *Mastering Veeam Backup & Replication*, we'd love to hear your thoughts! Scan the QR code below to go straight to the Amazon review page for this book and share your feedback.

https://packt.link/r/1837630097

Your review is important to us and the tech community and will help us make sure we're delivering excellent quality content.

Download a free PDF copy of this book

Thanks for purchasing this book!

Do you like to read on the go but are unable to carry your print books everywhere?

Is your eBook purchase not compatible with the device of your choice?

Don't worry, now with every Packt book you get a DRM-free PDF version of that book at no cost.

Read anywhere, any place, on any device. Search, copy, and paste code from your favorite technical books directly into your application.

The perks don't stop there, you can get exclusive access to discounts, newsletters, and great free content in your inbox daily

Follow these simple steps to get the benefits:

1. Scan the QR code or visit the link below

https://packt.link/free-ebook/9781837630097

2. Submit your proof of purchase
3. That's it! We'll send your free PDF and other benefits to your email directly

Part 1:
Installation – Best Practices, Core Architecture, and Other Enhancements

The objective of this section is to teach you about the best practices and optimizations for installing and upgrading Veeam. This section will also include core architectural changes and **Scale-Out Backup Repository (SOBR)** enhancements. It also covers the tape server and other enhancements within Veeam. You will be able to apply the best practices and optimizations to your installation of Veeam, as well as learn about the new enhancements.

The following chapters are included in this section:

- *Chapter 1, Installation – Best Practices and Optimizations*

- *Chapter 2, Core Architecture Enhancements*

- *Chapter 3, Scale-Out Backup Repository – What's New*

- *Chapter 4, Tape Server and Other Enhancements*

Installation – Best Practices and Optimizations

Veeam Backup & Replication v12 is part of the **Veeam Availability Suite**, the newest release for Veeam, and allows you to back up all your workloads, including **cloud**, **virtual**, **physical**, and **applications**. As we have seen from previous versions, it is simple yet flexible to meet your most challenging environment needs. This chapter will discuss how to install and upgrade the software, what components make up Veeam Backup & Replication v12, and some *best practices* and *optimizations*. There will be practical examples throughout this chapter of optimizing specific elements that make up the **Veeam** environment. We will also touch on some websites, such as the *Best Practices Guide for Veeam*, to give you resources to help you set up Veeam in your environment. As they say about Veeam – *"It Just Works."*

In this chapter, we're going to cover the following main topics:

- Understanding the best practices and optimizations for Veeam installation
- Configuring and optimizing Proxy Servers
- How to set up Repository Servers for success
- Understanding the Scale-Out Backup Repository (SOBR)
- Upgrading Veeam Backup & Replication to v12

Technical requirements

To ensure a successful installation, you will require the following:

- You must have Windows Server 2019/2022 deployed with the necessary disk space to install the application (**2012/2008 R2 SP1** is also currently supported). **Windows 10** and other modern **Windows** desktop operating systems are also supported. Please see the following website for the operating system requirements: `https://helpcenter.veeam.com/docs/backup/vsphere/system_requirements.html?ver=120#backup-server`.

- You must have downloaded the latest **ISO file** from `www.veeam.com`, which requires registering on the site and allows you to obtain a trial license. At the time of writing, version `12.0.0.1420` is the current release.

- *Veeam Best Practices* website: `https://bp.veeam.com/vbr/`.

- Veeam documentation website: `https://helpcenter.veeam.com/docs/backup/vsphere/overview.html?ver=120`.

Understanding the best practices and optimizations for Veeam installation

Installing **Veeam Backup & Replication v12** is a straightforward process. Setting up Veeam, if not done right, can lead to components not working correctly and poor performance, among other things. It will protect your data and environment with minimal configuration when set up correctly. This section will go through the installation process and touch on the best practices and optimizations for your environment.

Installing Veeam Backup & Replication v12

Before installing **Veeam Backup & Replication v12**, you must ensure that you have a server deployed, based on the *Technical requirements* in the preceding section, with enough disk space for the installation.

> **Note**
> Veeam will configure the default backup repository on the drive with the most available disk space, whether it's the OS drive, Application drive, or Catalog drive.

As a best practice for installing Veeam, the disk layout should be similar to the following so that you can separate components to ensure the best possible performance:

- **OS drive**: This is where your operating system resides and should be used only for this.

- **Application drive**: This will be your application installation drive for Veeam and all its components.

- **Catalog drive**: Veeam uses a catalog that can generate around 10 GB of data per 100 VMs backed up with file indexes. If this will be a significant storage requirement for your deployment, it may be advisable to allocate *the Catalog folder* to a separate drive.

Once your server is ready and you have downloaded the **ISO file** and mounted it, follow these steps to install Veeam:

1. Run the `setup.exe` file on the mounted ISO drive:

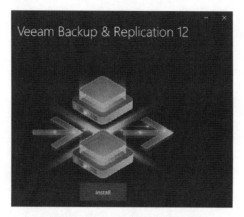

Figure 1.1 – Main installation screen

2. Click on **Install Veeam Backup & Replication**:

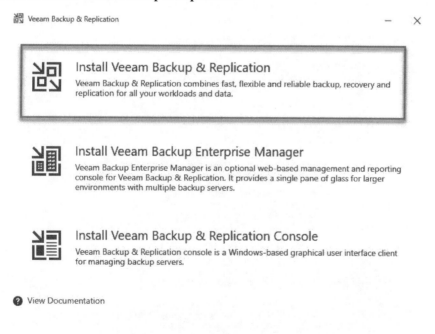

Figure 1.2 – Veeam Backup & Replication install option

3. You will see the **License Agreement** window at this point. You must click **I Accept** to continue:

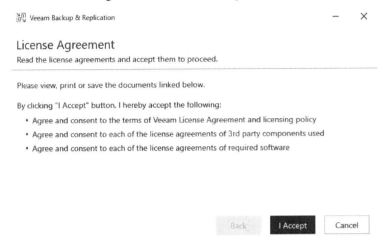

Figure 1.3 – License Agreement

4. You will now need to provide a valid license file, whether you've purchased it or it's a trial; if you do not have this at this stage of the installation, you can click **Next** to continue, and Veeam will operate in the *Community (Free) Edition*. When you obtain the license file, you can install that within the application under the menu and **License**:

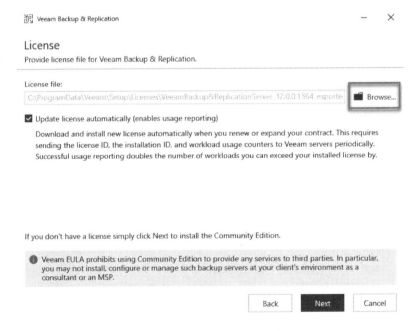

Figure 1.4 – License dialog window

5. After clicking **Next**, the installer will do a system check for any required prerequisites. Should something be missing, you will be prompted and have the option to install the missing components:

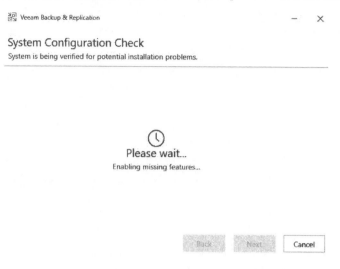

Figure 1.5 – System Configuration Check – missing components

6. Once all the components get installed, you will be taken to the following screen. Unlike in previous Veeam Backup & Replication versions, this screen does not allow you to input a user account to run the services. Instead, with v12 of Veeam, you need to select the **Customize Settings** link:

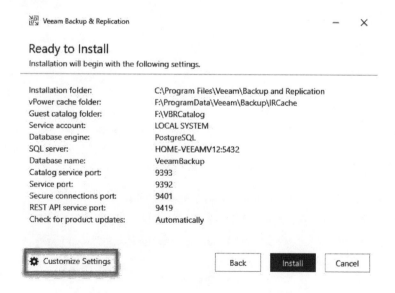

Figure 1.6 – Option to specify different settings

> **Note**
>
> Under the default configuration, you will see a new option for using PostgreSQL Server, which we will look at once the installation is completed.

7. You will now be able to enter a user account for the Veeam services, better known as a **Service Account**. There are some recommended settings for this service account:

    - You must have **Local Administrator** rights on the Veeam server.

    - If you are using a separate SQL Server and not the Express edition (Microsoft SQL Server 2016 SP2 Express edition) included as part of the Veeam installation, you will require permission to create the database. The same goes for the PostgreSQL option.

    - You will need full NTFS permissions to the folder containing the catalog.

    For more details about these permissions, please visit `https://helpcenter.veeam.com/docs/backup/vsphere/required_permissions.html?ver=120`:

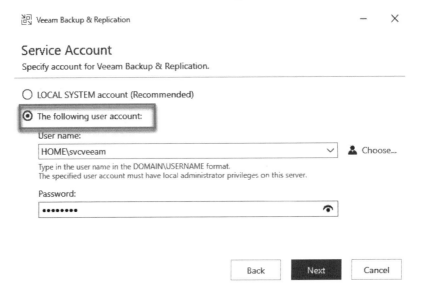

Figure 1.7 – Server user account

I am using an account I created on my lab server for this setup. In contrast, in a production scenario, you would already have a service account set up in Active Directory to enter at this stage.

8. You will now select your database options, including the required Windows or SQL credentials. Click **Next** to continue:

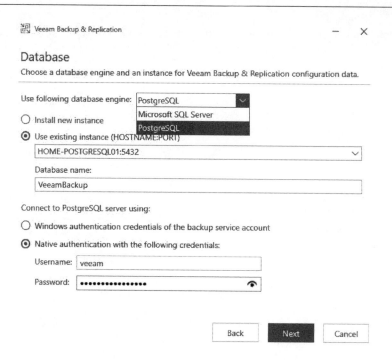

Figure 1.8 – Database server selection and credentials used

9. The following screen allows you to change the installation locations for the installation components. Click **Next** once you have completed this part of the installation:

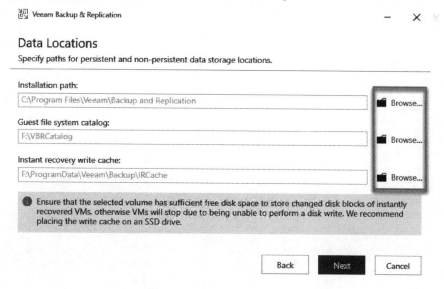

Figure 1.9 – Installation paths for the application

10. You will then be prompted for the **Port Configuration** properties to be used. You can leave them as their defaults. Then, click **Next**:

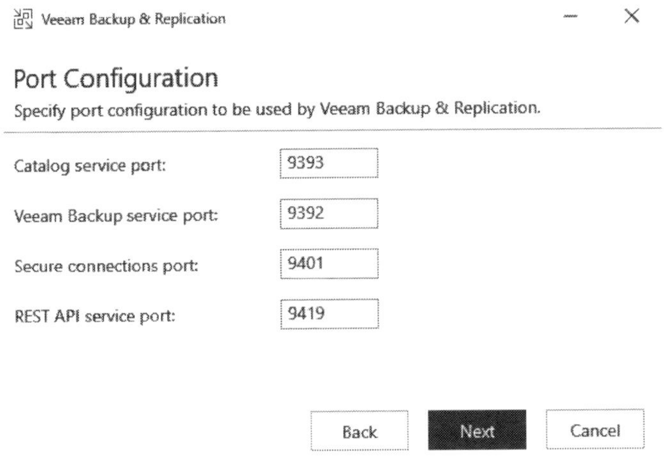

Figure 1.10 – Port Configuration selection

With the release of Veeam Backup & Replication v12, you can now use a different database type – *PostgreSQL*. This choice allows users to transition from Microsoft SQL, which requires licensing (SQL Express does not but has a 10 GB limit for the database size), but PostgreSQL does not because it is open source. The PostgreSQL database can be installed directly on the Veeam Backup Server or any other database server, such as Windows or Linux. For more details on PostgreSQL, please see the *Further reading* section at the end of this chapter.

You can now complete the installer by installing the local PostgreSQL Server instance and then the application. Veeam will also set the user account you selected to start all the services:

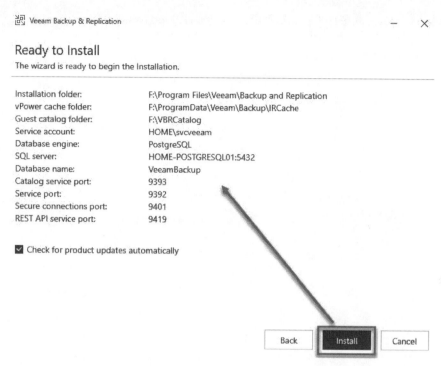

Figure 1.11 – Ready to Install – checking for updates

1. Click **Install** to proceed with the installation and start setting up the components that work together with the backup server.

> **Note**
>
> PostgreSQL Server 14.5 will be installed during the installation, but at the time of writing, the latest release is 15.1.

2. You will see the installation progress dialog after clicking **Install**:

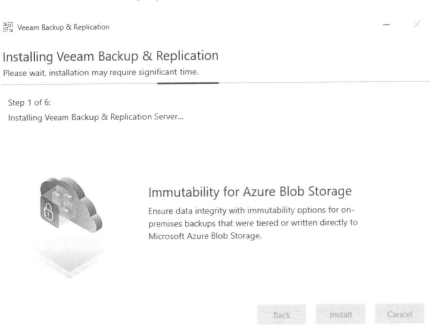

Figure 1.12 – Installation progress

3. Once complete, you can click **Finish** to complete the installation:

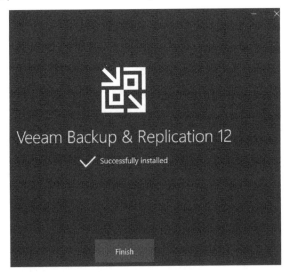

Figure 1.13 – Installation complete

Now, let's start configuring the required settings for Veeam to work with VMware:

- **Repository Server**: The server that gets used for storing the backup files.

- **Proxy Servers**: The servers that perform all the backup tasks.

- **VMware vCenter Credentials**: This is used to connect and see your clusters, hosts, vApps, and virtual machines. vCenter server is not required as standalone ESXi hosts are also supported if licensed in VMware.

4. When you first launch the **Veeam Backup & Replication** console, you will be taken directly to the **Inventory** tab, and **Virtual Infrastructure** will be in focus:

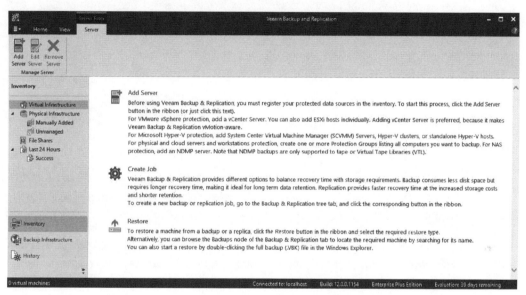

Figure 1.14 – Initial console screen

5. This screen is where we will begin adding the Virtual Center so that you can start backing up your virtual machines. Click on the **ADD SERVER** option to begin this process. You will then be prompted to select what kind of server you wish to add. Choose **VMware vSphere** and then either **vSphere** or **vCloud Director**:

Figure 1.15 – vSphere or vCloud Director selection

You would typically select vSphere here; however, if you have vCloud Director in your environment, you may also want to choose this option. When you choose **vSphere**, you will be prompted for two things to complete the connection:

- The DNS or IP address of your vCenter server (*DNS is the preferred method*).

- **Credentials**: This can either be a `vsphere.local` user or a domain account that got set up for access. You are also able, at this point in the wizard, to add credentials to the Veeam console using the **Add** button.

6. Enter the required credentials, click **Next**, and then click **Apply** to complete the VMware vSphere setup. You will now see your vCenter server listed under the **Virtual Infrastructure** section of the console and can browse the hosts and virtual machines.

Now, let's look at the next piece required for the infrastructure: the **Proxy server**. By default, the **Veeam Backup & Replication** server is your **VMware Backup Proxy** and **File Backup Proxy**. Due to my lab's limitations, I will use this server as an example, but in the real world, you would add multiple Proxy servers to your environment for better performance and as per best practices. Also, based on best practices, you would typically disable the Veeam Backup & Replication server as the Proxy Server to allow the other Proxy Servers to handle the workload.

The next component you will require is a **Repository Server**, which is the location where Veeam Backup & Replication will store your backup files. By default, Veeam Backup & Replication creates a **Default Backup Repository**, typically on the biggest drive attached to your backup server. This location will be where the **Configuration Backups** usually get backed up to. There are multiple options for adding a repository:

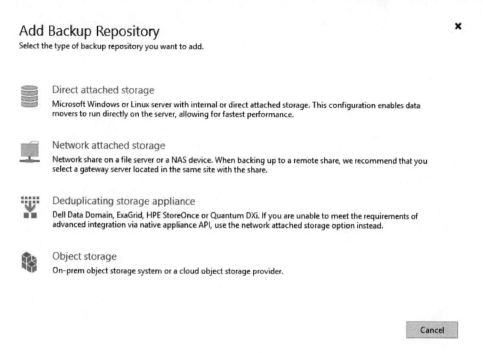

Figure 1.16 – Add Backup Repository selection

The first three selections are for block storage. At the same time, the last one is **Object storage**, which can now be used for backups directly due to the enhancement in v12 and can be part of a Scale-Out Backup Repository as any of the tiers – **Performance**, **Capacity**, and **Archive** for offloading data.

> **Note**
>
> Offloading data happens with the **Capacity** and **Archive** tiers.

Direct to Object is a new feature that was introduced with Veeam Backup & Replication v12. It allows users to move away from block storage and send their data directly to object storage, whether on-premises or in the cloud, with one of the many vendors such as Azure, AWS, Wasabi, and so on. The feature also allows you to use Object in the Performance Tier of a **SOBR**, of which you can use multiple object storage extents, but they have to be from the same vendor. You cannot mix them with Azure and AWS as both would need to be either one to be an acceptable configuration.

The following is a backup job configured to go to a SOBR with object storage as the Performance tier:

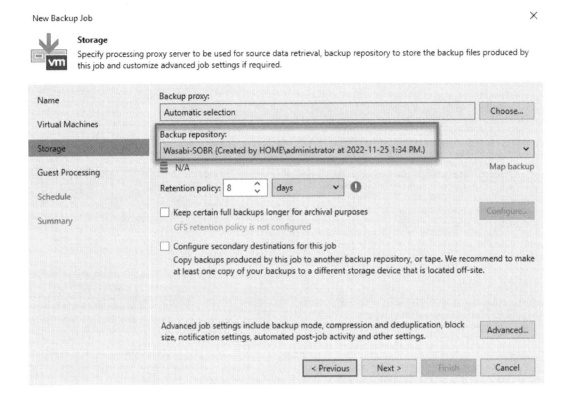

Figure 1.17 – Backup job using SOBR with Direct to Object storage

The following screenshot shows SOBR configured with Wasabi object storage under **Performance Tier**:

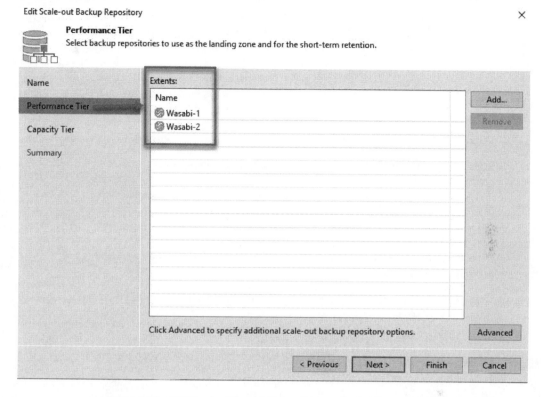

Figure 1.18 – SOBR using Wasabi Object Storage for Performance Tier

You have now installed and completed the basic configuration required for **Veeam Backup & Replication**. We will now look at how to optimize **Proxy Servers** and **Repository Servers**.

Configuring and optimizing Proxy Servers

Proxy Servers are the workhorses of the Veeam Backup & Replication v12 application, and they do all the heavy lifting or processing of tasks for backup and restore jobs. When you set up Veeam, you need to ensure that the Proxy Servers are configured as per best practices:

- `https://bp.veeam.com/vbr/VBP/2_Design_Structures/D_Veeam_Components/D_backup_proxies/vmware_proxies.html`

- `https://helpcenter.veeam.com/docs/backup/vsphere/backup_proxy.html?ver=120`

Introduced in Veeam Backup & Replication v12 is the ability to use Linux proxies in conjunction with **Continuous Data Protection (CDP)** and a standard proxy like in the previous version, v11a. This is another way for companies to move away from having to license a Windows Server and use one of the many Linux distributions. Not all Linux versions are supported, as noted here: `https://helpcenter.veeam.com/archive/backup/120/vsphere/system_requirements.html#vmware-backup-proxy-server`.

When you decide to deploy a Proxy server, Veeam Backup & Replication will install two components on the server:

- **Veeam Installer Service**: This gets used to check the server and upgrade software as required
- **Veeam Data Mover**: This is the processing engine for the Proxy server and does all the required tasks

Veeam Backup & Replication Proxy Servers use a **transport mode** to retrieve data during backup. Three standard modes are available, and they are listed in order, starting with the most efficient method:

- **Direct Storage Access**: The proxy is placed in the same network as your storage arrays and can retrieve data directly.
- **Virtual Appliance**: This mode mounts the VMDK files to the Proxy server for what we typically call **Hot-Add Mode** to back up the server data.
- **Network**: This mode is the least efficient but will be used when the previous methods are unavailable. It moves the data through your network stack. It is recommended not to use 1 GB but instead 10 GB.

In addition to these standard transport modes, which are provided natively for VMware environments, Veeam provides two other transport modes: **Backup from Storage Snapshots** and **Direct NFS**. These provide storage-specific transport options for NFS systems and storage systems that integrate with Veeam.

Refer to the integration with storage systems guide for more details: `https://helpcenter.veeam.com/docs/backup/vsphere/storage_integration.html?ver=120`.

Along with the transport modes, there are specific tasks that the Proxy server performs:

- Retrieving the VM data from storage
- Compressing data that's being backed up
- Deduplicating data blocks so that only one copy is stored
- Encrypting data in transit and backup files
- Sending the data to the backup Repository Server (backup job) or another backup proxy server (replication job)

Veeam Proxy Servers leverage what is known as VMware **vStorage APIs – Data Protection** (formerly known as **VMware vStorage APIs for Data Protection or VADP**) when using all transport modes other than Backup from Storage Snapshots and Direct NFS.

It would be best if you considered the following regarding your Proxy Servers:

- **Operating system**: Most software vendors will always recommend the latest and greatest, so if you choose Windows, choose 2022. Alternatively, you can select Linux using the newest release (for example, *Ubuntu 22.04.1 LTS*). For Linux VMware, backup proxies support all transport modes as of Veeam Backup & Replication v11a and support being a CDP Proxy in v12.

- **Proxy placement**: Depending on the transport mode for the server, you will need to place it as close to the servers you want to back up, such as on a specific host in VMware. The closer to the source data, the better!

- **Proxy sizing**: This can be tricky to determine and will depend on the physical or virtual server. Veeam Proxy Servers complete **tasks** where one virtual disk is processed for a VM or one physical disk is processed for a server. Therefore, Veeam recommends one physical core or one vCPU and 2 GB of RAM per task.

Veeam has a formula for calculating the required resources for a Proxy server:

- **D**: Source data in MB
- **W**: Backup window in seconds
- **T**: Throughput in MB/s = D/W
- **CR**: Change rate
- **CF**: Cores required for a full backup = T/100
- **CI**: Cores required for an incremental backup = (T * CR)/25

Based on these requirements, we can use a data sample to perform the calculations:

- 500 virtual machines
- 100 TB of data
- An 8-hour backup window
- 10% change rate

Using these numbers, we can perform the following calculations:

We can use the numbers we calculated to determine the required amount of cores needed to run both full and incremental backups to meet our defined SLA.

Based on our calculations and considering that you require 2 GB of RAM for each task, you need a virtual server with 36 vCPUs and 72 GB of RAM. This size may seem like a considerable server, but keep in mind that it uses sample data. Your calculations will likely be much smaller or more extensive, depending on your dataset.

Should you use a physical server as a Proxy, you should have a server with two to 10 core CPUs. In the case of our sample data, two physical servers are what you require. If you are using virtual servers for proxies, the best practice is to configure them with a maximum of 8 vCPUs and add as many as needed for your environment – in this case, you would need five servers.

Should you want to size things based on incremental backups only, your requirements are less than half the full backup sizing – 15 vCPUs and 30 GB of RAM.

There are limitations for Proxy Servers that you need to be aware of when it comes to job processing and performance. As we noted previously, a Proxy server performs **tasks**, which are assigned CPU resources. Concurrent task processing depends on the resources available in your infrastructure and the number of Proxy Servers you have deployed. As shown in the following screenshot, when it comes to adding a Proxy server to Veeam Backup & Replication, there is the **Max concurrent tasks** option, which correlates to the number of CPUs that are assigned:

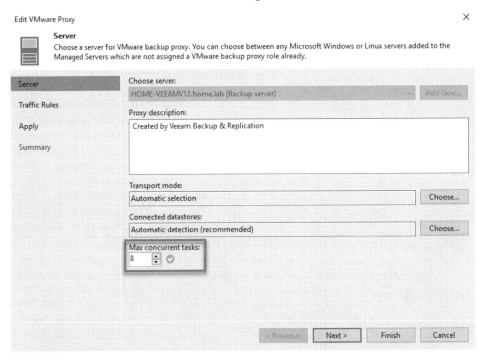

Figure 1.19 – Max concurrent tasks limitation for Proxy Servers

Task limits can be found at `https://helpcenter.veeam.com/docs/backup/vsphere/limiting_tasks.html?ver=120`.

> **Important note**
>
> Job performance will be impacted based on the tasks of a Proxy server. For example, if you had a Proxy server with 8 CPUs and added two virtual machines for backup, one with four disks and another with six disks, the Proxy server would process only eight of the 10 disks in parallel. The remaining two disks would have to wait on resources before being backed up in previous versions of Veeam.

With Veeam Backup & Replication v12, when you add a new Proxy server, it will have the concurrent tasks set automatically based on the number of CPUs/vCPUs that the physical or virtual server has. So, in the case of my lab, the Veeam server has four vCPU, so it got configured with eight concurrent tasks. Yes, this does not follow the sizing rule, but Veeam allows two times the number of CPUs/vCPUs for the concurrent task count.

You should now be able to right-size your Proxy Servers in terms of the CPU and RAM and understand proxy placement and how it processes tasks. Proxy Servers process and send data to Repository Servers, which is the focus of the next section.

How to set up Repository Servers for success

A Repository Server is a storage location for your backups, so setting them up right the first time will ensure you have the best performance. When creating a repository, it is always a good idea to follow the Veeam Backup & Replication best practices: `https://bp.veeam.com/vbr/VBP/2_Design_Structures/D_Veeam_Components/D_backup_repositories/`.

The following are some things to consider when setting up a repository:

- **ReFS/XFS**: With Windows 2019/2022, ensure you format your repository drive(s) as ReFS with 64k block sizing to take advantage of space savings for Synthetic Fulls and GFS. For Linux, you need to set up XFS and Reflink to take advantage of space-saving and Fast Cloning. In both of these situations, storage efficiency will be realized for Synthetic Full backups. This efficiency prevents duplication but is not deduplication.

- **Sizing**: Ensure that you adhere to the Veeam Backup & Replication recommendation of one core and 4 GB of RAM per repository task. Just like Proxy Servers, your Repository servers have task limits as well. At a minimum, you need two cores and 8 GB of RAM.

When calculating the sizing requirements, you need to consider your Proxy Servers and the amount of CPU configured; you then need to use a 3:1 ratio for the core count on a Repository Server.

Example: Your Proxy Server is configured with 8 CPUs; you need to configure the Repository Server with 2 CPUs based on this rule of 3:1. To configure the RAM, you must multiply the CPU count by four to end up with 8 GB of RAM.

When you use the Windows ReFS filesystem as your repository, you must consider the overhead required for the filesystem and add another 0.5 GB of RAM per terabyte of ReFS.

Setting up your task limits for a Repository Server differs from a Proxy server due to how tasks get consumed. The setting you choose will be handled differently:

- **Per-VM Backup Files**: When selected in Veeam Backup & Replication v12, this creates a backup chain per VM located in a job; rather than having a chain for all VMs together, they get separated, so each VM has its chain with a VBM, a VBK, and VIB files. Therefore, if the backup job has 10 virtual machines, it will consume 10 repository tasks and 10 proxy tasks.

  For comparison, here's an example of a v11a backup chain with one VBM (metadata file), the initial VBK (full backup file), and the VIB file (incremental backup file):

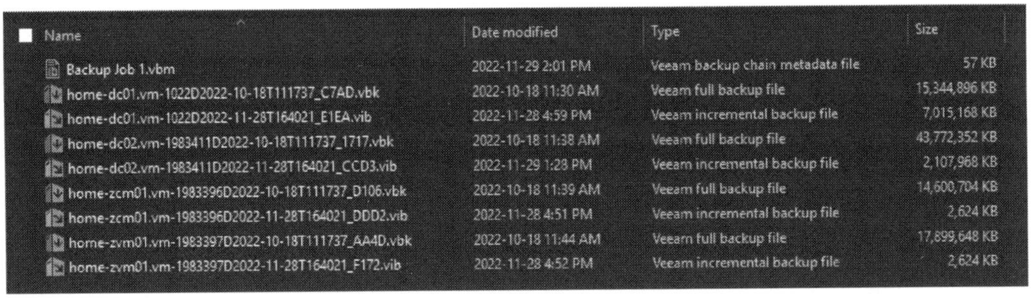

Figure 1.20 – Per VM backup chain in v11

  Now, here's an example of the new Per VM backup chain from v12 where each VM will have separate VBM, VBK, and VIB files:

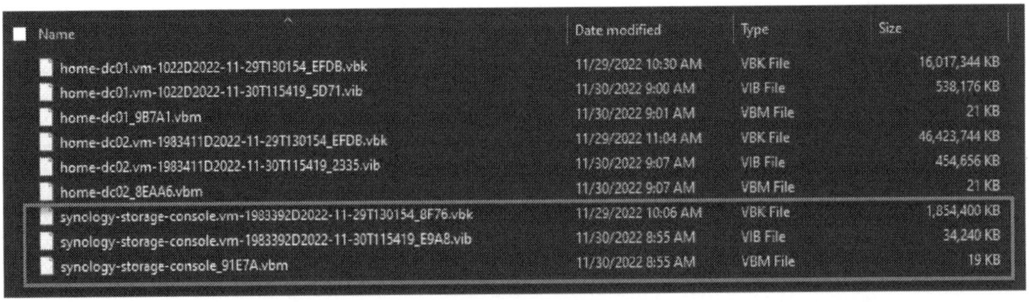

Figure 1.21 – Per VM backup chain in v12

- **No Per-VM Selection**: The backup job consumes one repository task, and the proxy task will remain the same with one task per virtual disk.

> **Note**
>
> To find out more about task limits, go to `https://helpcenter.veeam.com/docs/ backup/vsphere/limiting_tasks.html?ver=120`.

When you're setting up a repository for the first time, you can set the task limit:

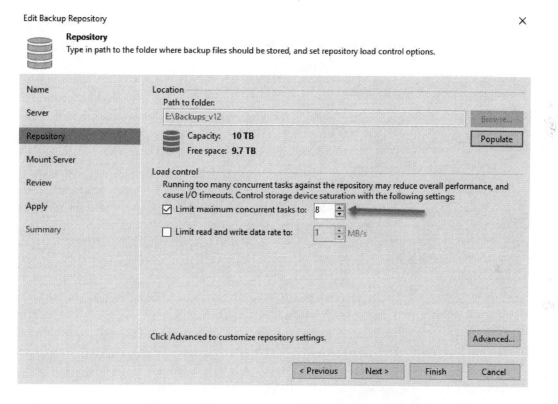

Figure 1.22 – Repository task limit

> **Important note**
>
> When you limit the number of tasks per repository and have jobs with many virtual machines requiring backups, this will be one of the bottlenecks in your environment. You also need to ensure that you do not set the limit too high, as that could overwhelm your storage, causing performance degradation. Make sure you test all your components and the resources available for your backup infrastructure.

After completing this section, you should be able to choose which type of filesystem you wish to use for your repository and size it correctly based on your CPU and RAM. We also discussed the per-VM versus no per-VM methods, including the new v12 per-VM chains and how they get created. We will use this knowledge to tie this into creating a Scale-Out Backup Repository.

Understanding the Scale-Out Backup Repository

So, what is a **SOBR** you ask? A **SOBR** uses multiple backup repositories, called performance extents, to create a sizeable horizontal scaling repository system. Veeam Backup & Replication can use multiple repositories of various types, such as the following:

- **Windows Backup Repositories**: NTFS or the recommended ReFS.
- **Linux Backup Repositories**: XFS with Reflink.
- **Object Storage**: Direct to object storage. This is now available in v12 for us to use for all tiers of a SOBR, including the Performance Tier.
- **Shared Folder**: **NFS**, **SMB**, or **CIFS**.
- Deduplication storage appliances.

SOBR can expand with on-premises storage such as block storage, object storage, or a cloud-based object repository known as a Capacity Extent. Veeam Backup & Replication combines the **Performance** extents, **Capacity** extents, and **Archive** extents into one to summarize their capacities:

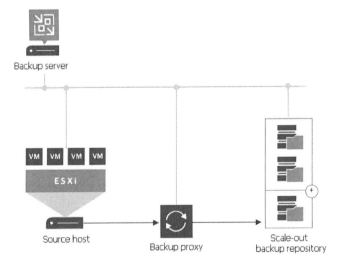

Figure 1.23 – Scale-Out Backup Repository

The ability to use a SOBR is dependent on the license version that you use with Veeam Backup & Replication:

- **Enterprise**: Allows for a total of two SOBRs with three active extents and unlimited inactive extents
- **Enterprise Plus & VUL (Veeam Universal License)**: Provides an unlimited number of SOBRs with as many performance extents needed but only one Capacity/Archive Tier per SOBR

> **Tip**
>
> Should you downgrade your licensing from Enterprise Plus or Enterprise to Standard, you will lose the ability to target your jobs to the SOBR. You can, however, restore data from the SOBR.

The different license types limit you in the number of SOBRs and extents per SOBR you can configure. As we noted previously, there is a limit of two for **Enterprise** and an unlimited number for **Enterprise Plus/VUL**.

> **Tip**
>
> For the best performance and manageability, it is best to keep your SOBR limited to three to four extents if possible. If you are using object storage, then one of the components of the SOBR will be the Capacity Tier.

The SOBR works with many types of jobs or tasks in Veeam Backup & Replication:

- Backup jobs
- Backup copy jobs
- VeeamZIP jobs
- Agent backups – Linux or Windows agent v2.0 or later
- NAS Backup jobs
- Nutanix AHV backup jobs
- Veeam Agent for Mac
- Veeam backups for Amazon and Microsoft Azure (via backup copy jobs)

The next thing to keep in mind is the limitations of using a SOBR, as there are certain things you cannot do:

- Only Enterprise, Enterprise Plus, and VUL licenses can be used
- You cannot use it as a target for configuration backup jobs, replication jobs, VM copy jobs, Veeam Agent v1.5 or earlier for Windows, or v1.0 Update1 or earlier for Linux

- Adding a repository as an extent to a SOBR will not be allowed if there is an unsupported job using the repository
- Rotating drives are not supported
- You are unable to use the same extent in two SOBRs

Please refer to the following limitations page on the Veeam Backup & Replication website for more details: `https://helpcenter.veeam.com/docs/backup/vsphere/limitations-for-sobr.html?ver=120`.

When it comes to the makeup of the SOBR, there are three tiers:

- **Performance Tier**: Fast storage and fastest access to data can now include object storage, whether on-premises or cloud-based, in v12
- **Capacity Tier**: Typically, this is object storage for archival and offloading capabilities
- **Archive Tier**: Additional object storage for long-term archival and infrequently accessed objects

> **Note**
>
> When adding object storage as the Performance Tier, you must ensure that each one added is of the same vendor. For example, if the first Performance Tier you add is from Wasabi, the subsequent extents must also be Wasabi-based as you cannot add something such as Amazon S3. This will be crucial in planning if you decide to start using object storage in a SOBR.

For the performance tier, you will want to ensure it has the fastest storage, block, or object storage so that when access to files and restores is required, it is as fast as possible. When you create a standard repository before adding it to a SOBR, specific settings are retained in the SOBR:

- The number of simultaneous tasks it can perform
- The storage read and write speeds
- The data decompression settings on the storage
- The block alignment settings of the storage

The SOBR will not inherit a repository backed by rotating drives. If you choose to use the Per-VM backup option, this is on by default in a SOBR.

> **Note**
>
> If you decide to use cloud-based object storage, keep in mind that it will not be the same as using block storage or on-premises object storage as it will need to pull data from the cloud back to on-premises, which could slow restoration down.

Something else to think about is the backup file placement policy that you will use. There are pros and cons to both, and specific operating systems, such as ReFS and XFS, require one over the other. The two types of placement policies are as follows:

- **Data locality**
- **Performance**

Please refer to the *Performance Tier* page on the Veeam Backup & Replication website for more information: `https://helpcenter.veeam.com/docs/backup/vsphere/backup_repository_sobr_extents.html?ver=120`.

Data locality allows the scale-out to place all backup files in the chain to the same extent within the SOBR, keeping files together. In contrast, the Performance policy will enable you to choose which extents to use for both full backup files (VBK) and incremental files (VIB).

For further information on backup placement, see this Veeam Backup & Replication page: `https://helpcenter.veeam.com/docs/backup/vsphere/backup_repository_sobr_placement.html?ver=120`.

Now, when it comes to the Capacity Tier, there can only be one per scale-out, and it is required to be one of the options shown in the following screenshot:

Figure 1.24 – Object Storage options for the Capacity Extent

> **Note**
>
> These same object storage options for the Capacity Tier apply to the Performance Tier now and, as noted, have to be the same for each extent you want to add to the Performance Tier.

Using a Capacity Tier as part of your SOBR is suitable for the following reasons:

- You can tier off older data when your SOBR reaches a specific percentage capacity to allow you to free up storage space.

- Company policy stipulates you keep a certain amount of data onsite. Then, all older data is tiered off to the Capacity Tier after *X* days.

- Using it falls into the 3-2-1-1-0 rule, where one copy of the information is offsite. See this blog post for more details on the 3-2-1-1-0 rule: `https://www.veeam.com/blog/3-2-1-rule-for-ransomware-protection.html`.

You specify the Capacity tier after creating it as a standard repository, during the SOBR wizard:

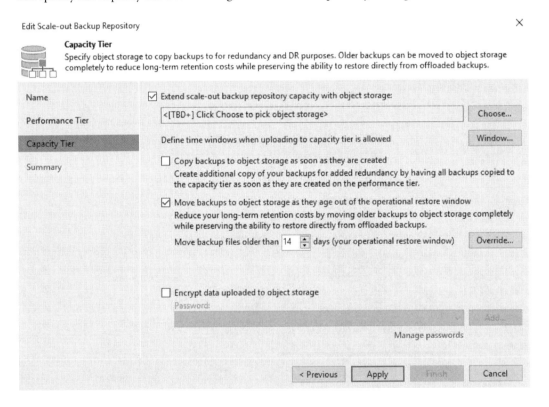

Figure 1.25 – Capacity Tier of the Edit Scale-out Backup Repository wizard

Please visit the *Capacity Tier* page on the Veeam Backup & Replication website for more information: `https://helpcenter.veeam.com/docs/backup/vsphere/capacity_tier.html?ver=120`.

We will now tie everything we've learned together and create a SOBR. First, you will need to open the Veeam Backup & Replication console and select the **BACKUP INFRASTRUCTURE** section at the bottom left. Then, click on the **Scale-out Repositories** option on the left:

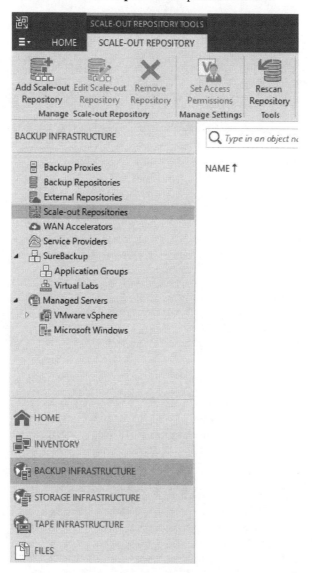

Figure 1.26 – The Scale-out Repositories section of the console

Once you're in this section, you can either click the **Add Scale-out Repository** button in the toolbar or, on the right-hand pane, right-click and select **Add Scale-out backup repository…**.

At this point, you must name the SOBR and give it a thoughtful description; the default name is **Scale-out Backup Repository 1**. Then, click **Next** to go to the **Performance Tier** section of the wizard:

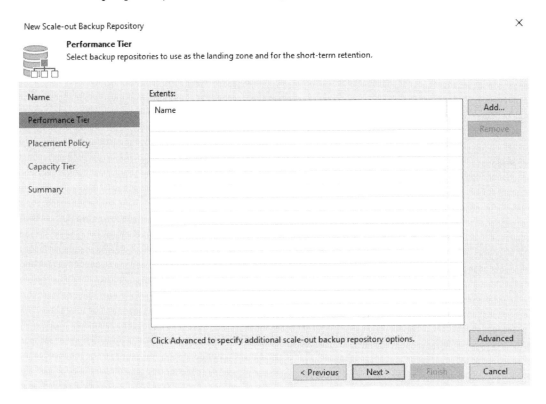

Figure 1.27 – The New Scale-out Backup Repository wizard – Performance Tier

In this section, click the **Add…** button and choose the standard repositories that will be part of your SOBR. You can also click on the **Advanced** button to choose two options:

- **Use per-VM backup files (recommended)**
- **Perform a full backup when the required extent is offline**

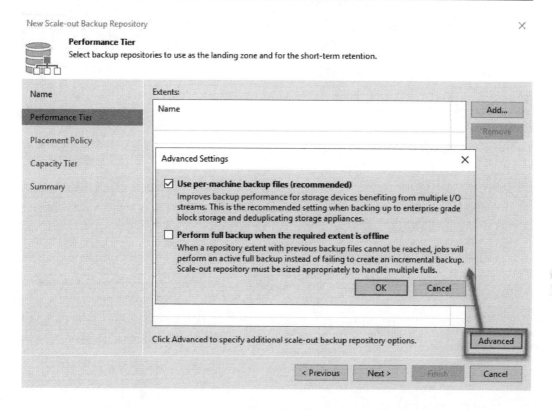

Figure 1.28 – Advanced settings for the Performance Tier area of SOBR

Click the **Next** button to proceed. At this point, you must pick your placement policy – **Data Locality** or **Performance**. As we mentioned, if you're using ReFS or XFS, you must select **Data Locality** to take advantage of each operating system's storage savings. Click **Next** after making your choice.

You can now choose to use **Capacity Tier** for your SOBR or click the **Apply** button to finish. Note that when you select a Capacity Tier, there are several options you can enable:

- Copy backups to object storage as soon as they get created in the Performance Tier.

- Move backups to object storage as they age out of the restore window. The default is 14 days. You can also click the **Override** button to specify offloading until the space required is below a certain percentage.

- You can also encrypt your data upload to the object storage as another level of security:

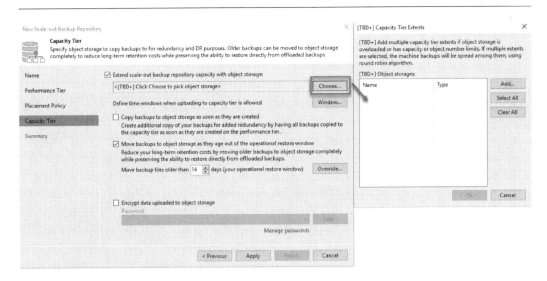

Figure 1.29 – Capacity Tier selection for Scale-out

Note that some Capacity Tier targets support immutability. This feature is an essential attribute in the war on ransomware. In v12, Capacity Tier targets that support immutability include AWS S3 with object lock and S3-compatible object storage systems.

Please see the Veeam Readiness program to determine whether your object storage is supported here: `https://www.veeam.com/alliance-partner-technical-programs. html?programCategory=ready-object-immutable`.

Once complete, you will see your new SOBR. When you select it, you will see the performance tier extents and the Capacity Tier if you chose it:

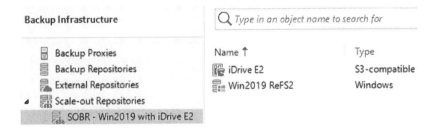

Figure 1.30 – SOBR created

For further information on the SOBR, visit this Veeam Backup & Replication page: `https:// helpcenter.veeam.com/docs/backup/vsphere/sobr_add.html?ver=120`.

The final thing to discuss is how to manage the SOBR after creating it. Once created, you may need to do any of the following:

- Edit its settings to change the performance policy, for example.
- You may need to rescan the repository to update the configuration in the database.
- Extend the performance tier by adding another extent to the SOBR.
- Put an extent in maintenance mode to perform maintenance on the server that holds it or evacuate the backups to remove the extent.
- Switch an extent into **Sealed Mode**, where you do not want any more writes to it but can still restore from it. This process allows you to replace the extent with a new one.
- Run a report on the SOBR.
- Remove an extent from the SOBR, which requires maintenance mode, evacuate, and remove.
- Remove the SOBR altogether.

Two other new things with Veeam Backup & Replication v12 for managing SOBR and repositories, in general, are the **VeeaMover** and **SOBR Rebalance** options. Both of these features are new to v12 and will be covered in *Chapter 3, Scale-Out Backup Repository – What's New*, but a brief overview follows.

VeeaMover

VeeaMover is a built-in utility that simplifies operations for moving data between repositories and VMs between jobs. It allows you to move from ReFS to ReFS while keeping the block clone savings (a similar thing happens with XFS too). You can also move from NTFS to ReFS to take advantage of the block clone savings in ReFS. Also, moving VMs from one job to another is realized with VeeaMover.

SOBR Rebalance

When you use a SOBR with multiple extents, depending on your placement policy, some of the extents fill up more than others. There is now a new feature called SOBR Rebalance, which helps with this by spreading backups across the extents. This operation does require an outage; however, moving the files around and depending on their size, this could take some time.

As noted, we will cover more of the VeeaMover and SOBR Rebalance in *Chapter 3*.

Once set up within Veeam Backup & Replication v12, the SOBR is pretty self-sufficient. Still, there are maintenance tasks that you need to do to ensure optimal performance and plenty of storage is available for backups.

For more information on SOBR management, please visit the following page on the Veeam Backup & Replication website: `https://helpcenter.veeam.com/docs/backup/vsphere/managing_sobr_data.html?ver=120`.

Upgrading Veeam Backup & Replication to v12

This section will discuss the process required to upgrade your existing **Veeam Backup & Replication** environment to **v12**. If you have Veeam Backup & Replication v10 installed, you can proceed with the following steps to conduct the upgrade.

> **Important note**
>
> If you have **Veeam Enterprise Manager** installed on your server, you will be prompted to upgrade this before upgrading Veeam Backup & Replication.

Once your server is ready and you have downloaded the *ISO file* and mounted it, follow these steps to upgrade your server and components:

1. Run the `setup.exe` file on the mounted ISO drive:

Figure 1.31 – Main installation screen – Upgrade

2. Click on the **Upgrade** button to proceed.

3. You will be prompted to click on the component to upgrade – in this case, **Upgrade Veeam Backup & Replication**:

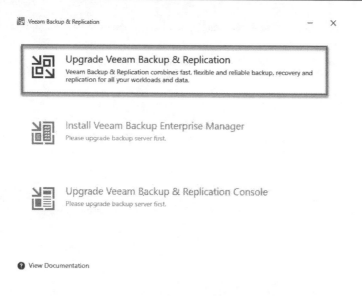

Figure 1.32 – Upgrade selection

> **Note**
>
> If Veeam Backup Enterprise Manager were on your server, you would be prompted to upgrade this before you could upgrade Veeam Backup & Replication.

4. After clicking **Veeam Backup & Replication**, the upgrade installation will proceed.

5. The **License Agreement** dialog is the next thing you will see. Here, click **I Accept** to proceed:

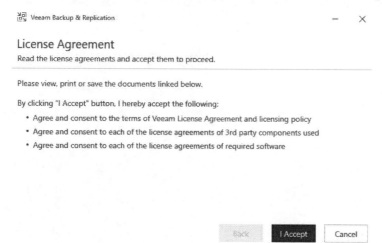

Figure 1.33 – License Agreement dialog

6.   After accepting the license agreement, you will be presented with the **Upgrade** dialog, which shows the components to be upgraded with the current and new versions. You can also check the **Update remote components automatically** option so that they are upgraded on console launch:

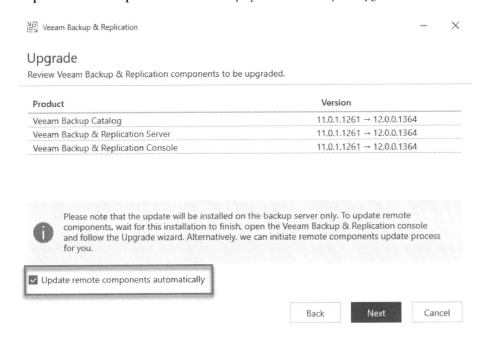

Figure 1.34 – Upgrade dialog with components

7.   After clicking **Next**, the next screen you'll see is the **License** dialog. This is where you can use the **Browse…** button to enter your license and then click **Next** to proceed:

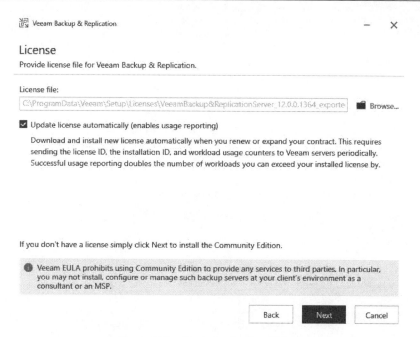

Figure 1.35 – License selection dialog

8. The installer will now performs a system check and enable any missing features required for the installation to continue:

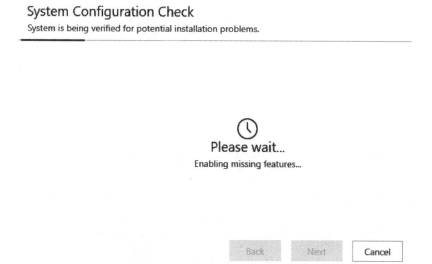

Figure 1.36 – System Configuration Check

9. Now, you'll be on the **Service Account** screen, which you will use for the Veeam Backup &
    Replication services to run under. In my case, I am using a **LOCAL SYSTEM** account, which
    is the Administrator. However, to follow best practices, you should create a service account
    ahead of time. Click **Next** to proceed after entering the required account information:

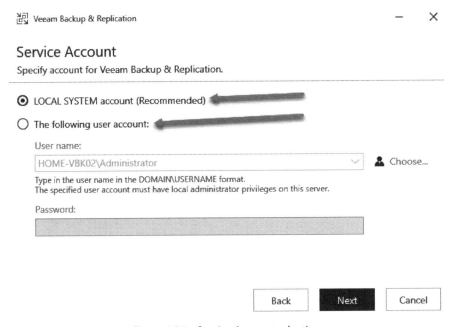

Figure 1.37 – Service Account selection

10. The next screen is the **Database** dialog, which will detect your current installation and ask you to verify the connection settings. You should also follow best practices and have a login account created on your database server; in this case, SQL Server is using my Windows login credentials, a small deployment. Click **Next** after validating the settings:

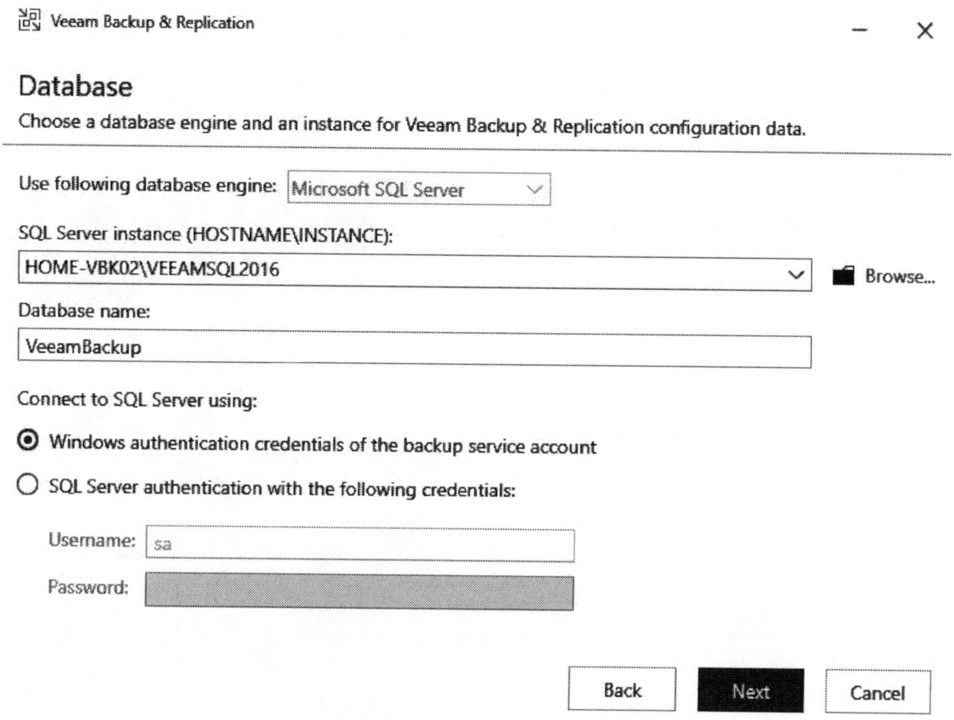

🖳 Veeam Backup & Replication   — ✕

Database

Choose a database engine and an instance for Veeam Backup & Replication configuration data.

Use following database engine: | Microsoft SQL Server ⌄ |

SQL Server instance (HOSTNAME\INSTANCE):

| HOME-VBK02\VEEAMSQL2016   ⌄ | 📁 Browse...

Database name:

| VeeamBackup |

Connect to SQL Server using:

◉ Windows authentication credentials of the backup service account

○ SQL Server authentication with the following credentials:

Username: | sa |

Password: | ▒▒▒▒▒▒▒▒▒▒▒ |

[Back] [Next] [Cancel]

Figure 1.38 – Database validation

11. You will be warned about the database being upgraded after clicking on **Next**. Be sure to click **Yes** to proceed:

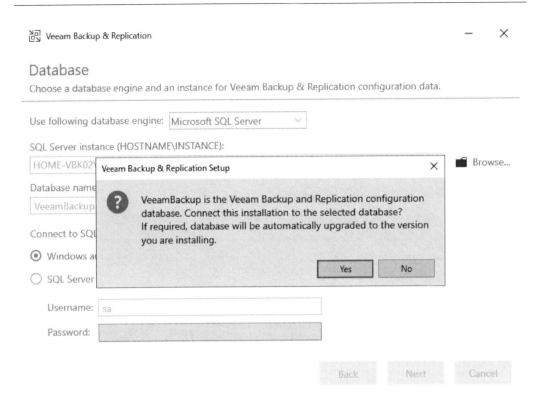

Figure 1.39 – Database upgrade warning

12. At this point, a **Configuration Check** process will be performed to ensure there are no incompatibilities for the upgrade and highlights them if there are any so that they can be resolved before you proceed with the upgrade. Click **Next** to proceed:

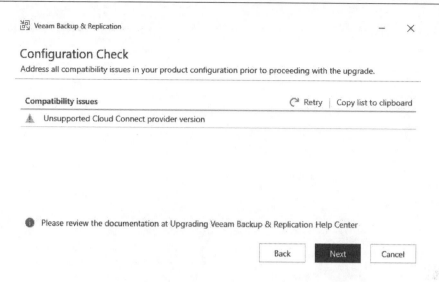

Figure 1.40 – Configuration Check for incompatibilities

> **Note**
>
> In my case, I have my Veeam Backup & Replication server pointed to a Service Provider record that is not compatible due to still being at v11. This check will allow users that have a Veeam Cloud connect to a Service Provider to see that they have not upgraded and be able to pause their upgrade until the Service Provider upgrades their side first. I proceeded with the upgrade for this book.

13. You will now see the **Ready to Upgrade** dialog. Click the **Upgrade** button to proceed:

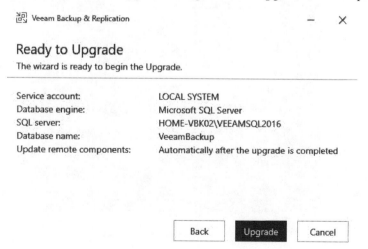

Figure 1.41 – Ready to Upgrade dialog

14. The next dialog you'll see is the progress dialog, which shows six steps that must be done to complete the upgrade:

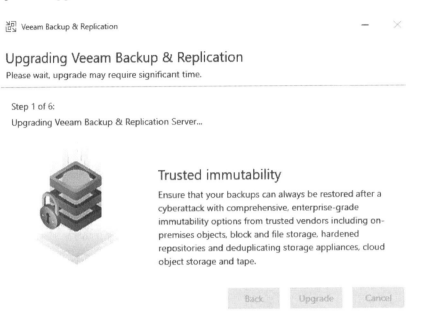

Figure 1.42 – Upgrade progress

15. After the progress dialog finishes, the upgrade will be complete, and you can click **Finish**:

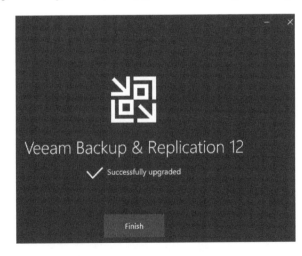

Figure 1.43 – Upgrade completed

The upgrade process is now complete, and your jobs should continue to run as scheduled. You will now have the option to upgrade your backup chains to the *Per-VM Backup Chains*, which are new within Veeam Backup & Replication v12.

You can do this upgrade in the console by going to the **Home** tab and selecting **Backups**. Right-click on the backup job and select **Upgrade backup chain format**:

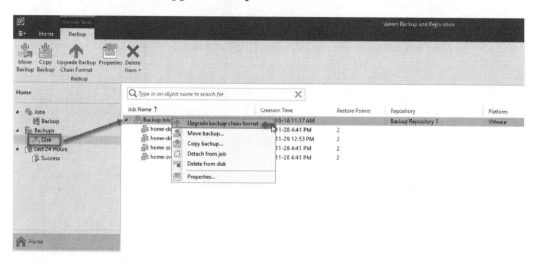

Figure 1.44 – Upgrade backup chain format

As shown in *Figure 1.21*, the layout of the new files for each server has VBM (metadata) and backup files (VBK/VIB).

After you select **Upgrade backup chain format**, you will be prompted with a dialog to proceed. Click **OK**. A status window will appear, showing the progress of the upgrade:

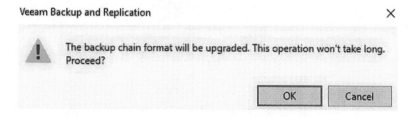

Figure 1.45 – Backup chain upgrade proceed dialog

After you click **OK**, you will see the progress dialog and the upgrade upon completion:

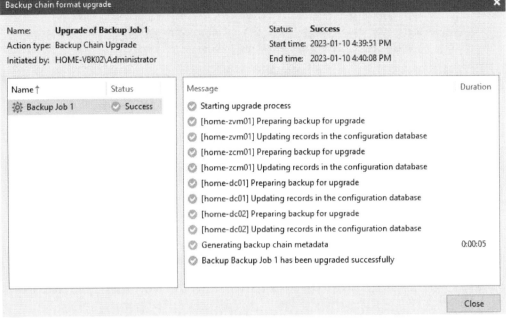

Figure 1.46 – Backup chain format upgrade progress

With that, we have covered installing and upgrading the backup chain format to the new *Per-VM backup chains*. I will now summarize the lessons learned in this chapter.

Summary

This chapter provided you with the tools required to install Veeam Backup & Replication v12 and the components that make up the installation. We discussed the prerequisites, including the versions of SQL Server or PostgreSQL that you can use – Express or SQL Standard/Enterprise and PostgreSQL locally installed with Veeam or a remote instance on Windows/Linux. Then, we addressed how to set up Proxy Servers, the configuration best practices, and optimal settings. This part was then followed by a discussion on repositories and how to create them and included best practices and optimizations for best performance. Afterward, we looked at Scale-Out Backup Repositories and how to set them up, including the Performance Tier and the Capacity Tier, and how to manage them once they've been set up. Lastly, we looked at the upgrade process for Veeam Backup & Replication to update an existing instance from version 11a to 12 and convert the backup chains into the new Per-VM backups.

This chapter should have helped ensure that you have all the basics covered. The next chapter will cover many core architecture changes within Veeam Backup & Replication v12.

Further reading

To learn more about the topics that were covered in this chapter, take a look at the following resources:

- Veeam Community Edition: `https://www.veeam.com/virtual-machine-backup-solution-free.html`

- PostgreSQL Server: `https://www.postgresql.org/`

- An Object Storage Repository in Veeam: `https://helpcenter.veeam.com/docs/backup/vsphere/object_storage_repository.html?ver=120`

- Backup Proxies: `https://helpcenter.veeam.com/docs/backup/vsphere/backup_proxy_requirements.html?ver=120`

2

Core Architecture Enhancements

This chapter will cover many new core architecture enhancements in the Veeam Backup and Replication v12 software. You will learn about the new option of using a PostgreSQL server as your database instead of Microsoft SQL Server, which can be a replacement or even an upgrade to your current SQL server. We will also look at the new per-VM backup chain changes, which will make a backup administrator's life easier from a management and troubleshooting perspective. Lastly, we will look at some new Linux features, such as an option for a hardened repository in the wizard and using Linux as a proxy, including CDP.

In this chapter, we're going to cover the following main topics:

- Introducing a PostgreSQL server for your database
- Understanding per-VM backup changes
- Learning about the Linux hardened repository option in the repository wizard
- Exploring new Linux proxy roles

Technical requirements

One of the main requirements will be to already have a **Veeam Backup and Replication** setup to follow some examples given in the following sections. If you followed *Chapter 1*, you have all the required prerequisites.

Introducing a PostgreSQL server for your database

With the release of Veeam Backup and Replication v12, another database option has been introduced – a **PostgreSQL server**. All previous Veeam Backup and Replication versions were Microsoft SQL Server installations, whether it was SQL Server Express (LocalDB) or directing the installation to a full-blown SQL server (Standard or Enterprise). Within v12, both are available for your deployment – SQL Server or PostgreSQL.

Those reading and hearing about a PostgreSQL server for the first time might ask how it differs from Microsoft SQL Server. The most significant difference is that PostgreSQL is an open source relational database. In contrast, SQL Server requires licensing to be able to use it unless you use the free SQL Express edition, which is limited to a 10 GB file size limit and one socket, or four CPU cores. Another differentiating factor is that the PostgreSQL server is not just bound to a Microsoft Windows machine and can also be deployed on Linux, which helps companies save on server licensing.

You can select **PostgreSQL Server** during the installation of Veeam Backup and Replication v12, as shown in the following screenshot:

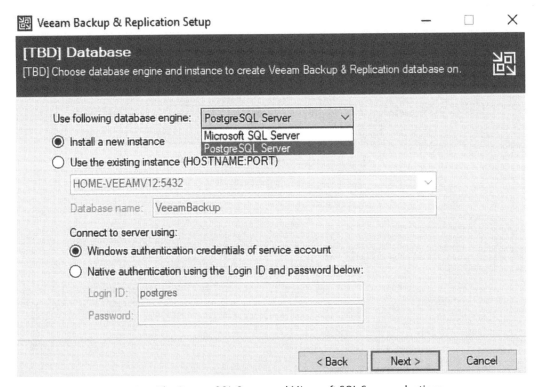

Figure 2.1 – The PostgreSQL Server and Microsoft SQL Server selections

Once you have selected **PostgreSQL Server**, you will see the following in the installation wizard:

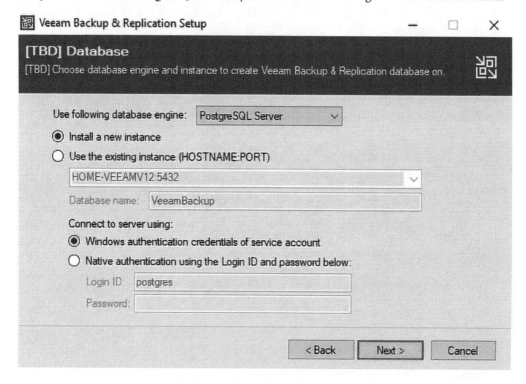

Figure 2.2 – PostgreSQL Server selected

It is here that you will see the different options:

- **Install a new instance**: This will install the PostgreSQL server on the same server on which you are installing Veeam Backup and Replication v12

- **Use the existing instance (HOSTNAME:PORT)**: This is where you can direct the installer to use a current deployment of the PostgreSQL server on either a Windows or Linux server, including the port number

- **Connect to server using**: This allows you to connect to the PostgreSQL server using the Windows credentials for the service account or a native (local) user within the PostgreSQL server system

> **Note**
>
> Due to security, your database administrator may need to set up a PostgreSQL server account for you to use for connection purposes ahead of your installation. The user will require the **CREATEDB** role within the PostgreSQL server.

Veeam Backup and Replication v12 will install PostgreSQL Server 15 locally if you choose to have an all-in-one server, but the most recent version of PostgreSQL is 15.1 at the time of writing. The following shows the installation of the PostgreSQL server:

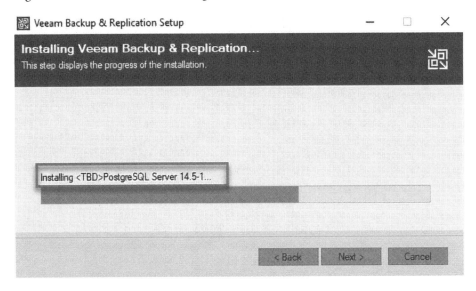

Figure 2.3 – The PostgreSQL server being installed during the VBR setup

As well as having PostgreSQL as a new option for the database, there is a migration path from SQL Server to move your databases to the PostgreSQL server. The backup server and **Enterprise Manager** (**EM**) must have the same database type, as the configuration restore to PostgreSQL requires the same database version.

You must upgrade to Veeam Backup and Replication v12 first, and then migrate:

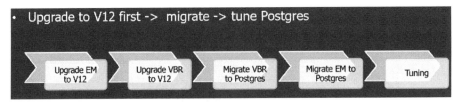

Figure 2.4 – The migration path from SQL Server to the PostgreSQL server

Some of the benefits of moving from SQL Server to the PostgreSQL server are as follows:

- A lower cost to do business – there's a reduction in licensing fees from Microsoft/SQL

- No CPU or DB size restrictions

- It embraces Linux for backend services

Now that we have looked at the newest database option for Veeam Backup and Replication v12, let's look at another updated feature with per-VM backup chains.

Understanding per-VM backup changes

When it comes to setting up your repositories, whether standard or a **Scale-Out Backup Repository** (**SOBR**), you have the option to select **Use per-machine backup files**, as shown in the following screenshot:

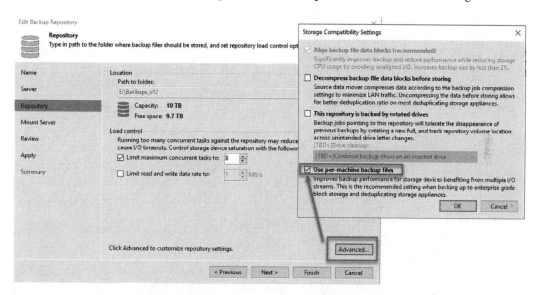

Figure 2.5 – Selecting the Use per-machine backup files option

This option should be selected for your backups, the same as in Veeam Backup and Replication v11, and it is selected by default in Veeam Backup and Replication v12. Using this option takes advantage of multiple I/O streams to enterprise-grade storage arrays, allowing backups to process faster and write faster to disk.

Now, you might be asking yourself, if the option was there in Veeam Backup and Replication v11 and is still there in v12, what is the difference now when enabling this option? The difference now is in how files are stored on your repository servers compared to previous versions of Veeam.

There are three formats for storing files on a repository server:

- **Single storage**: This method is used when you do not select the **Use per-machine backup files** option in your repository configuration. The data is written to your repository using a single write stream, with everything saved into one file and one metadata file (. VBM) created. This backup type is depicted in the following diagram:

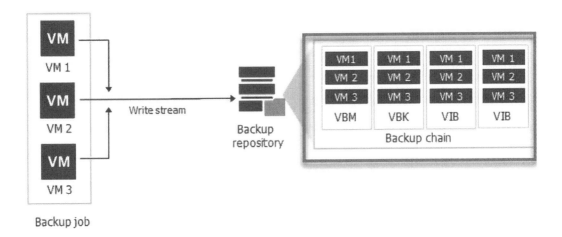

Figure 2.6 – A single storage backup chain

- **Per machine or split machine**: This is another method available before v12, and it still creates one metadata file (.VBM) but splits out the servers for the VBK (full backup files) and VIB (incremental backup files) as separate chains. This format was how per-VM backups worked before Veeam Backup and Replication v12, as shown in the following diagram:

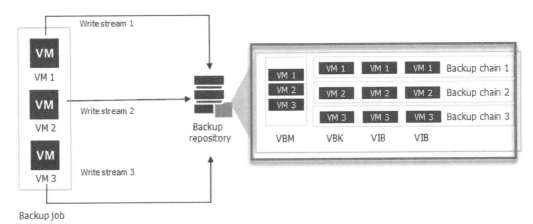

Figure 2.7 – Per-VM backup chains before v12

Another way to show the usage of per-VM backup chains before Veeam Backup and Replication v12 is shown in the following screenshot, from within File Explorer on the repository server:

Name	Date modified	Type	Size
Backup Job 1.vbm	2022-11-29 2:01 PM	Veeam backup chain metadata file	57 KB
home-dc01.vm-1022D2022-10-18T111737_C7AD.vbk	2022-10-18 11:30 AM	Veeam full backup file	15,344,896 KB
home-dc01.vm-1022D2022-11-28T164021_E1EA.vib	2022-11-28 4:59 PM	Veeam incremental backup file	7,015,168 KB
home-dc02.vm-1983411D2022-10-18T111737_1717.vbk	2022-10-18 11:38 AM	Veeam full backup file	43,772,352 KB
home-dc02.vm-1983411D2022-11-28T164021_CCD3.vib	2022-11-29 1:28 PM	Veeam incremental backup file	2,107,968 KB
home-zcm01.vm-1983396D2022-10-18T111737_D106.vbk	2022-10-18 11:39 AM	Veeam full backup file	14,600,704 KB
home-zcm01.vm-1983396D2022-11-28T164021_DDD2.vib	2022-11-28 4:51 PM	Veeam incremental backup file	2,624 KB
home-zvm01.vm-1983397D2022-10-18T111737_AA4D.vbk	2022-10-18 11:44 AM	Veeam full backup file	17,899,648 KB
home-zvm01.vm-1983397D2022-11-28T164021_F172.vib	2022-11-28 4:52 PM	Veeam incremental backup file	2,624 KB

Figure 2.8 – Per-VM backups before v12 shown in storage

- **True per machine**: This is the newest method for storing backups and is the default option when adding a repository to Veeam Backup and Replication v12. When you configure your repository and select the **Use per-machine backup files** option, you will get the new method to create a backup chain. This new method uses multiple I/O streams to write data for each workload (server) within the backup job. The data is saved to separate backup files and creates a separate metadata file (.VBM) for each backed-up server. This method is depicted in the following diagram:

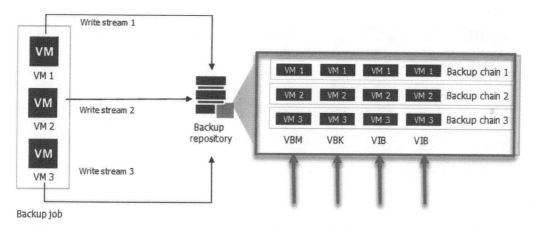

Figure 2.9 – True per-VM backup chains as introduced in v12

Another way to show the usage of true per-VM backup chains with Veeam Backup and Replication v12 is shown in the following screenshot, from within File Explorer on the repository server:

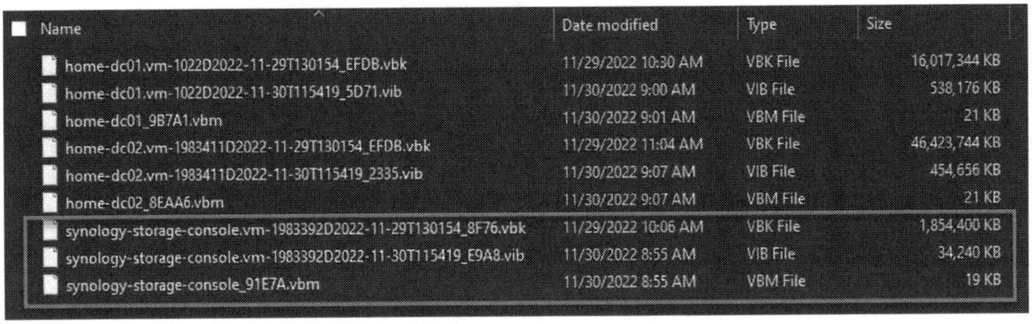

Name	Date modified	Type	Size
home-dc01.vm-1022D2022-11-29T130154_EFDB.vbk	11/29/2022 10:30 AM	VBK File	16,017,344 KB
home-dc01.vm-1022D2022-11-30T115419_5D71.vib	11/30/2022 9:00 AM	VIB File	538,176 KB
home-dc01_9B7A1.vbm	11/30/2022 9:01 AM	VBM File	21 KB
home-dc02.vm-1983411D2022-11-29T130154_EFDB.vbk	11/29/2022 11:04 AM	VBK File	46,423,744 KB
home-dc02.vm-1983411D2022-11-30T115419_2335.vib	11/30/2022 9:07 AM	VIB File	454,656 KB
home-dc02_8EAA6.vbm	11/30/2022 9:07 AM	VBM File	21 KB
synology-storage-console.vm-1983392D2022-11-29T130154_8F76.vbk	11/29/2022 10:06 AM	VBK File	1,854,400 KB
synology-storage-console.vm-1983392D2022-11-30T115419_E9A8.vib	11/30/2022 8:55 AM	VIB File	34,240 KB
synology-storage-console_91E7A.vbm	11/30/2022 8:55 AM	VBM File	19 KB

Figure 2.10 – A true per-VM backup chain as written to your repository

Refer to the *Further reading* section for links to the Veeam help site to explore the different backup types covered. Now that we have covered the new true per-VM backup option, let's look at another new feature – adding a Linux hardened repository to your backup infrastructure.

Learning about the Linux hardened repository option in the repository wizard

When Veeam Backup and Replication v11 was released, Veeam introduced the Linux hardened repository server, and now, with the release of Veeam Backup and Replication v12, the Linux hardened repository is an option you can select within the **Add Backup Repository** wizard when you choose the **Direct attached storage** option, as shown in the following screenshot:

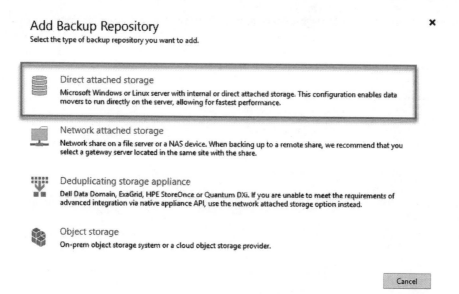

Figure 2.11 – The Add Backup Repository wizard and selecting Direct attached storage

Once you click the **Direct attached storage** option, you are presented with a new dialog, which contains **Linux (Hardened Repository)** as an option:

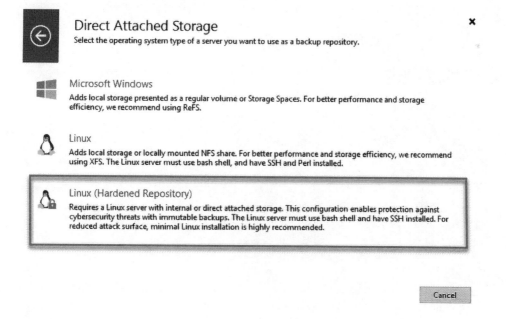

Figure 2.12 – The Linux (Hardened Repository) option directly in the wizard

After you select the **Linux (Hardened Repository)** option, you are presented with the option to add a new server or use an existing one if already set up in your environment, as shown in the following screenshot:

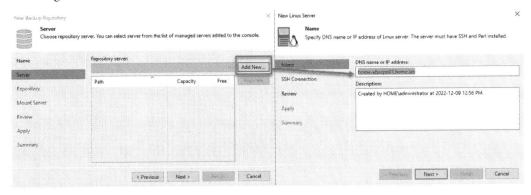

Figure 2.13 – Adding a new Linux hardened repository server

As you proceed through the **New Linux Server** wizard, you will be presented with the single-use credentials dropdown; you can either select a pre-existing one or add a new one to the system:

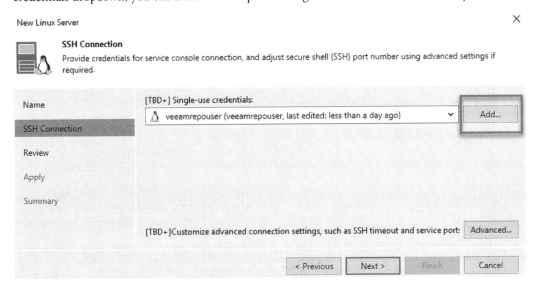

Figure 2.14 – A SSH connection, where we add a new single-use credential

Proceed through the **New Linux Server** wizard, and you will be returned to the **New Backup Repository** wizard to complete it. Once the Linux server is available, you pick the path to the immutable folder where the backups are stored and select or create a subfolder to store the backups. Once the wizard is completed, you will see the new Linux hardened repository in your list of repositories in the console:

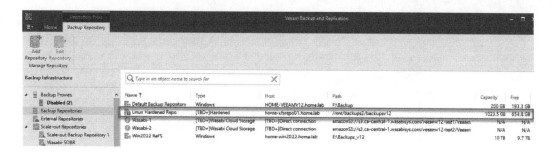

Figure 2.15 – The Linux hardened repository now configured for use

> **Tip**
> The Linux hardened repository can also be used as a proxy server using the NBD backup method, as there is no requirement for root access. This feature allows customers to use their hardware with more than one role on a server.

This completes our look at the new Linux hardened repository option now available in the Veeam Backup and Replication v12 repository wizard. Now, let's look at the final core enhancement – Linux proxy roles.

Exploring new Linux proxy roles

When it comes to using a Linux server as a proxy server, you can make this a physical server, or it can also be a VM. Access to a network where all servers can be backed up, along with access to storage, is beneficial no matter what you choose.

The evolution of the Linux proxy started in Veeam Backup and Replication v10, where you could use it as a standard proxy server using **HotAdd** mode for backups. Then, in Veeam Backup and Replication v11, additional modes were added:

- **NBD**: Network backup mode
- **Direct SAN**: Direct storage backup
- **HotAdd**: Attaches disks of the servers to the proxy for reading
- **Backup from storage snapshots (iSCSI and FC)**: Backups directly from your storage array based on your storage type

Along with the backup modes introduced in v11, the quick rollback (CBT restore) options allow you to restore a server using the latest backup and only restore the changed blocks. This feature is the quickest method for restoring a server.

Jumping forward to Veeam Backup and Replication v12, we now have even more enhancements for the Linux proxy roles. Along with all the roles available from v11, the newest proxy role to be added is the **Continuous Data Protection (CDP)** role, which will be covered in the final chapter of the book. Veeam CDP requires a source and target proxy server for it to function correctly, and this is why in Veeam Backup and Replication v12, you can now select a Linux server as a CDP proxy:

Figure 2.16 – The VMware CDP proxy selection to add a Linux server

After you click the **VMware CDP proxy** option, you need to click the **Add New…** button to select or add your new Linux CDP proxy:

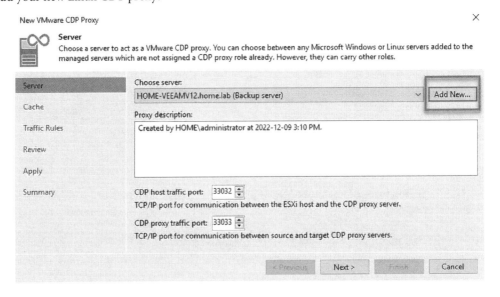

Figure 2.17 – Adding a new CDP proxy to specify the current or new Linux server

The following window is where you select **Linux** to add your server to the Veeam Backup and Replication v12 console:

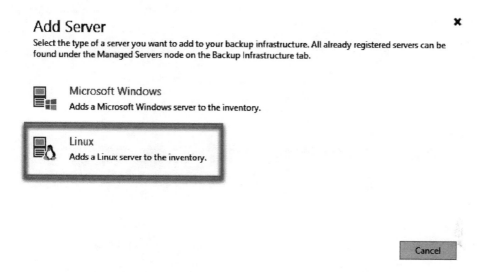

Figure 2.18 – Selecting the Linux server to add as a CDP proxy

You then complete the **New Linux Server** wizard to add the new Linux server to the CDP proxy wizard:

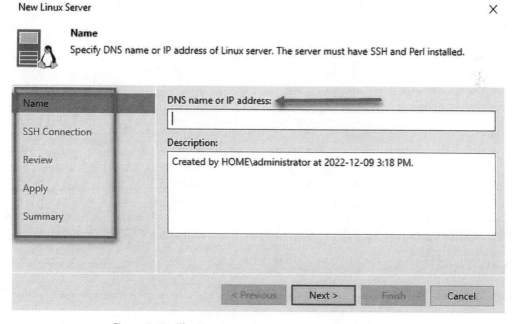

Figure 2.19 – The New Linux Server wizard for the CDP proxy

You then complete the **New VMware CDP proxy** wizard by selecting the cache folder and clicking on **Finish** to deploy the CDP proxy role software. It's recommended that the cache is on a drive with plenty of space. Once the wizard is complete, your new Linux CDP proxy will be added to the console.

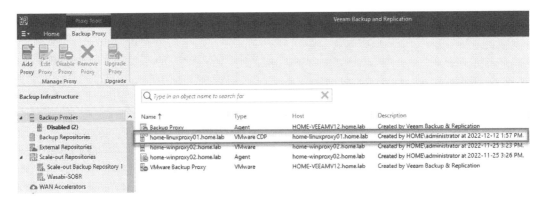

Figure 2.20 – The Linux CDP proxy added to the console

You then add a second CDP proxy (a source or destination, depending on the first deployment) to your environment to allow CDP to function correctly, as per the help site: https://helpcenter. veeam.com/docs/backup/vsphere/cdp_proxy.html?ver=120.

We have now covered the final topic of the chapter, with Linux proxy role enhancements for CDP.

Summary

This chapter has reviewed many of the new core enhancements to the Veeam Backup and Replication v12 software. We looked at the new PostgreSQL server database implementation, which can replace Microsoft SQL Server or be a fresh installation. We covered what is new with per-VM backup chains and how Veeam has implemented files per server in the backup repository. We looked at the new option when adding a repository for the Linux hardened repository, by making a selection in the wizard. Finally, we looked at the Linux proxy and all its new enhancements, including using it for CDP as a proxy.

Chapter 1 and *Chapter 2* covered Veeam Backup and Replication basics for installation, including best practices, optimization, and some new core enhancements to the product. The next chapter, *Scale-Out Backup Repository – What's New*, looks at more advanced and further features of Veeam Backup and Replication v12.

Further reading

- The PostgreSQL server: `https://www.postgresql.org/about/`

- Per-VM backup reference: `https://helpcenter.veeam.com/docs/backup/vsphere/per_vm_backup_files.html?ver=120`

- Linux proxy limitations and requirements: `https://helpcenter.veeam.com/docs/backup/vsphere/backup_proxy_requirements.html?ver=120#requirements-and-limitations-for-vmware-backup-proxy-on-linux`

- Linux CDP proxy reference: `https://helpcenter.veeam.com/docs/backup/vsphere/system_requirements.html?ver=120#vmware-cdp-proxy-server`

3

Scale-Out Backup Repository – What's New

The **Scale-Out Backup Repository** (**SOBR**) has gone through many additions, and with Veeam Backup & Replication v12, there are even more enhancements to make management more effortless. Users can now send backups directly to Object Storage with SOBR and have multiple buckets per SOBR tier, which we will explore later. In this chapter, we will look at a new technology called VeeaMover, which allows you to move backups from one extent to the other or even a new SOBR. VeeaMover also allows servers to move between jobs and repositories, which we will examine later. Lastly, we will look at the new SOBR Rebalance feature, which enables data between extents to balance space. We will also look at exporting data from all SOBR Tiers.

In this chapter, we're going to cover the following main topics:

- Understanding sending backup data direct to Object Storage with SOBR

- Exploring VeeaMover and its benefits

- Using SOBR Rebalance and exporting data

Technical requirements

For this chapter, having **Veeam Backup & Replication** is a requirement, along with access to an **Object Storage environment** to work with SOBRs. If you have been following along with this book, then you will know that *Chapter 1, Installation -- Best Practices and Optimizations*, covered the installation and optimization of Veeam Backup & Replication, which you will leverage in this chapter. Additionally, you can reference the SOBR section of the Veeam website: `https://helpcenter.veeam.com/docs/backup/vsphere/backup_repository_sobr.html?ver=120`.

Understanding sending backup data direct to Object Storage with SOBR

Within the Veeam Backup & Replication software, there are two types of repositories where you store your backups:

- **Standard repository**: This can contain many different options, but the newest one, **Object Storage (OBS - NEW)**, is the significant change to Veeam Backup & Replication v12, allowing direct-to-object storage for any of your jobs:

Figure 3.1 – Standard Object Storage repositories in Veeam Backup & Replication v12

- **Scale-Out repository**: This consists of standard repositories called *Extents* and can now contain the Object Storage standard repositories:

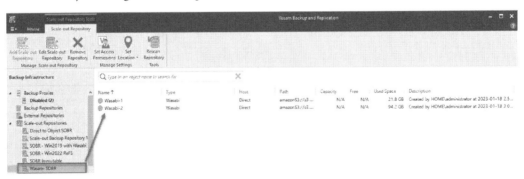

Figure 3.2 – Scale-out repository with Object Storage performance extents

SOBR allows you to scale support for different data tiers horizontally. It consists of one or more backup repositories called *Extents* and can be expanded using on-premises or cloud-based Object Storage in the Performance Tier. Everything in a scale-out repository gets joined into a system, and capacity gets summarized for the entire scale-out repository. The three types of Extents are as follows:

- **Performance**: This tier is typically local storage and the fastest to access for restoration and shorter retention
- **Capacity**: This tier is object storage and is used to send data when it reaches a certain threshold and for short-term archival purposes
- **Archive**: This tier is typically object storage but is where you send data that needs to be archived and doesn't need to be touched; is used for long-term archival purposes.

Some of the main benefits of the scale-out repository are as follows:

- Easy management of backup storage
- The ability to scale as required by adding more capacity with new extents
- Supports many backup targets, with the latest being OBS
- Allows granular performance policy setup – **Data Locality** or **Performance** mode

> **Note**
>
> When using Object Storage for the Performance Tier in the SOBR, the Data Locality or Performance policies do not apply in Veeam Backup & Replication v12.

- Provides unlimited cloud-based storage using capacity extent to offload data for long-term retention

Some of the many benefits of using Object Storage for your SOBR and performance tiers are as follows:

- **Capacity management**: Object Storage is effortless for scaling capacity versus traditional block storage, making it an easier choice for the performance tier
- **Immutability**: You can leverage immutable backups within Object Storage for your performance tiers, adding another layer of protection
- **Geo-redundancy**: Many Object Storage vendors can have the storage set up in a geo-redundant configuration, which will make a copy to another location from the primary site, giving you another layer for recovery

With Veeam Backup & Replication v12, some much-needed enhancements have been made to the scale-out repository, including the following:

- **Immutability for GFS**: You can now use the Immutability feature within the SOBR for any **Grandfather-Father-Son** (**GFS**) backups, which improves the files' security

- **Select Azure Cool Tier in Settings**: The ability to select Microsoft Azure cool tier storage during the setup for SOBR

- **Azure blob immutability support**: Microsoft Azure blob storage now contains the ability to have immutability

- **Wasabi integration in Wizard**: Wasabi is built into the SOBR configuration wizard natively

You can reference these enhancements and many others on the Veeam Backup & Replication website: `https://www.veeam.com/whats-new-availability-suite.html`.

We have now covered SOBR and how you can leverage Object Storage for all tiers – performance, capacity, and archive. We will now look at a new backend feature for moving data between repositories, VMs between jobs, and backup jobs to new storage: **VeeaMover**.

Exploring VeeaMover and its benefits

Moving backup files has been one of those things that has not been as easy as it should have been with Veeam Backup & Replication. Now, with the release of v12, a new under-the-hood feature called **VeeaMover** can help all backup administrators with these tasks. Imagine moving data from one Windows ReFS-backed repository to another Windows ReFS-backed repository while keeping the block cloning savings. Similar challenges currently exist when copying data between multiple XFS filesystems. Also, imagine migrating from a ReFS-backed repository to an XFS-backed repository or vice versa while maintaining block cloning savings built into those filesystems.

With VeeaMover, you can now move servers between jobs and even between repositories. Even the new SOBR Rebalance feature mentioned in the next section takes advantage of VeeaMover in the background.

Use cases for VeeaMover

There are some significant use cases for the use of the VeeaMover utility, and they are outlined as follows:

- **Migrating storage**: If you are looking to migrate your storage, whether from NTFS to ReFS, ReFS to ReFS, or ReFS to XFS and vice versa, this is a great use case for the VeeaMover utility. It allows you to move your backups from one repository to another and, in the case of ReFS to XFS or vice versa, will keep the block clone disk savings during the move.

The following screenshots show how you can move your backups from one storage to another. First, you need to navigate to the **Backups | Disk** section on the **Home** tab within the console, highlight the job you want to move to another storage repository, right-click, and select **Move backup…**:

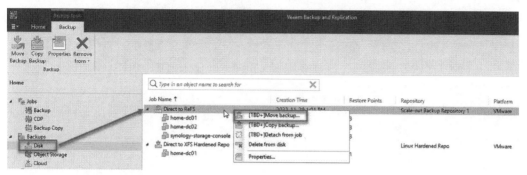

Figure 3.3 – The Move backup… option within the Disk section

After you select **Move backup…**, you will be presented with the following screen to confirm the move and set a **Destination repository option**:

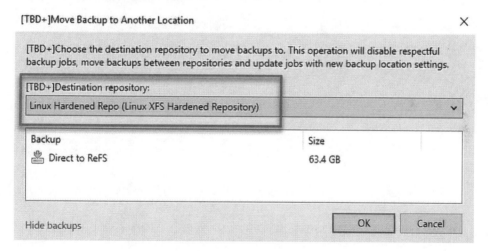

Figure 3.4 – Destination repository selection

> **Note**
>
> Take note of the information in this dialog as your backup jobs will be disabled during the move process between repositories. The backup job will be updated with the new repository once the data has been moved.

After clicking **OK**, the backup move process will start and display its progress, as follows:

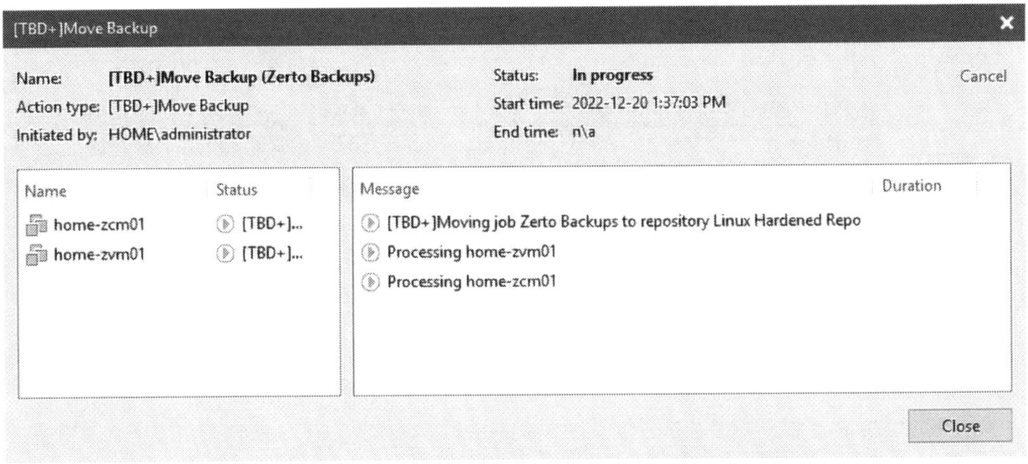

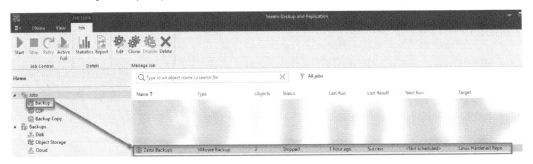

Figure 3.5 – Move Backup progress dialog

After completion, your job will be in the console and display the new repository as the location:

Figure 3.6 – Backup job moved to the new repository with VeeaMover

- **Migration to immutable storage**: The VeeaMover utility offers a useful solution, which allows backup administrators to move data from NTFS/ReFS over to immutable XFS repositories and allow jobs to use immutability going forward.

The following screenshot shows backups moving from a ReFS repository to a Linux XFS-hardened repository to use immutability:

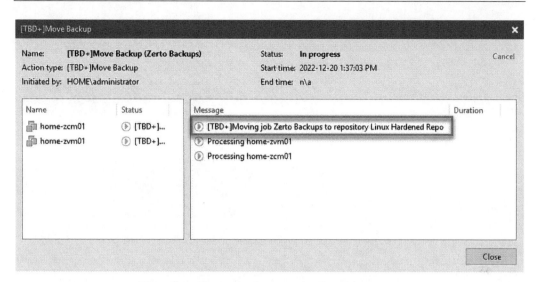

Figure 3.7 – Moving backups to a hardened repository

After the move, the result shows that the job is now pointing to the hardened repository and can now use the immutability feature:

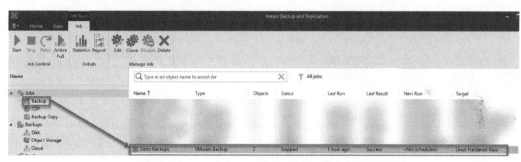

Figure 3.8 – Backup job has moved to the hardened repository

- **Moving VMs to new jobs**: The VeeaMover utility also allows you to migrate servers located in one backup job to another backup job, as well as storage. So, if you have a server that has been placed in the wrong job by accident, you can use VeeaMover to migrate it to the right job.

Navigate to the **Backups | Disk** section in the console and expand the backup job with the server you wish to move to another backup job. If you right-click on the server name, you will get the **Move backup…** option. Select it:

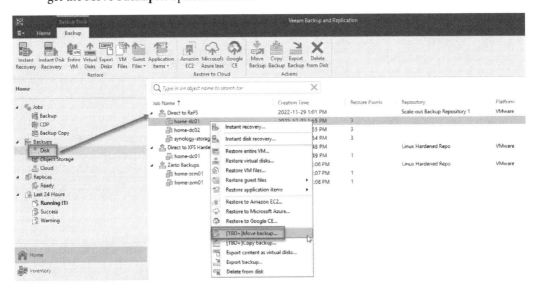

Figure 3.9 – Using the Move backup… option for a specific server in a backup job

You will then be prompted with another dialog to select the backup job you wish to move the server:

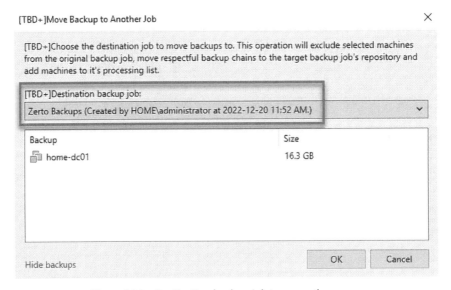

Figure 3.10 – Destination backup job to move the server

> **Note**
> Please note what will occur when moving a server from one job to another, as it will exclude the job from the current backup, move the backup chains to the target job's repository, and add the server to the new backup job selection list.

After clicking **OK** in the previous window, you will see a progress window pop up for moving the server to the new backup job:

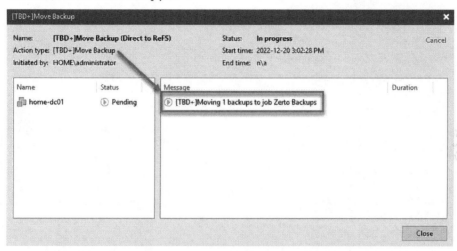

Figure 3.11 – Move backup job running

You will see that the server has been moved from one job to a new job within the console:

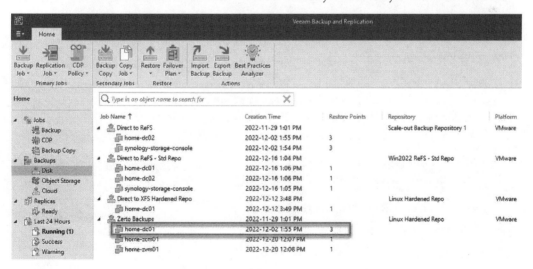

Figure 3.12 – Server moved to a new backup job

- **SOBR rebalancing**: The VeeaMover utility works in the background with the SOBR Rebalance feature, which will be discussed in this chapter's next section – *Using SOBR Rebalance and exporting data*.

As you can see, there are many use cases for VeeaMover and moving backups to new repositories or servers from one job to another. We will now explore the new SOBR Rebalance feature, which also takes advantage of VeeaMover in the background.

Using SOBR Rebalance and exporting data

One of the primary pieces of the Veeam Backup & Replication v12 infrastructure is its repository servers; however, using these repository servers to build a SOBR allows us to aggregate multiple standard repositories into one giant repository. The SOBR is comprised of Extents, which are the standard repositories. When you create a SOBR, and depending on how Veeam Backup & Replication chooses to use them based on your policy selection (**Data Locality** or **Performance**), some extents can get fuller than others.

Here are the placement policies:

- **Data Locality**: Backup chains are all stored in the same extent within the SOBR. This policy is selected when using both ReFS/XFS filesystems as it will use the block-cloning features of the respective filesystems.
- **Performance**: Full backup and incremental backup files are split across extents in this policy, and you will specify which extents are for which backup types. This policy does not work with block cloning in ReFS/XFS.

So, depending on which policy you have selected, how many extents you have in your SOBR, and how Veeam Backup & Replication determines how to use them, you can end up constantly managing space, but this is where the SOBR Rebalance feature comes into play.

So, what is SOBR Rebalance, you might be asking? Well, it is a process that can be invoked on a SOBR to redistribute storage across all performance extents, balancing the space used versus free space. However, it does require that you add a new extent to the SOBR before starting the process. This will ensure that it has sufficient free space to work on the SOBR, which should be considered good practice.

So, how does the Rebalance feature work for SOBRs? We'll cover the high-level steps here. If you want further details, please visit the link in the *Further reading* section:

1. After selecting the **SOBR Rebalance** option, the job starts.
2. A scan takes place to check the availability of the extents.
3. Extents determined to be available get placed in Maintenance Mode.
4. Backups are reviewed based on the SOBR placement policy.

5. Checks are made to see whether the storage will be out of "ideal free space," and the backup chains are analyzed from largest to smallest.

6. A search is done for the best extent for any data that needs to be moved to ensure compliance.

7. The rebalance scheduler will send a request for the preferred extent for placing the backups in the **Resource Scheduler** (**RTS**).

8. The rebalance job will perform tasks similar to those carried out by the extent job.

9. Once completed, the extents will exit Maintenance Mode.

To start the SOBR Rebalance process, you need to do the following:

1. Navigate to the **Backup Infrastructure** tab in the console.

2. Click on the SOBR located under **Scale-out Repositories** in the tree.

3. Hold down the *Ctrl* key on your keyboard while right-clicking on your SOBR.

4. From the menu, select **[TBD+]Rebalance** to start the process:

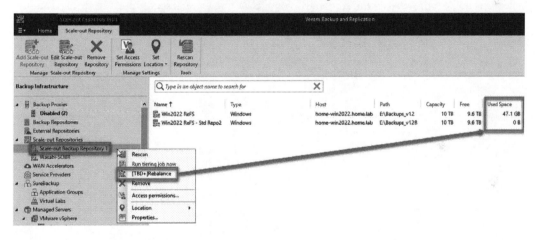

Figure 3.13 – Selecting the Rebalance option for a SOBR

If there is not enough space or an extra extent is required, as I noted in the preceding screenshot, you will see this error:

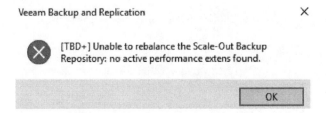

Figure 3.14 – Rebalance error due to no extent being available

If there is enough space and an extra extent has been added, then you will see the following dialog, where you can proceed with the rebalance:

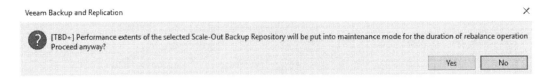

Figure 3.15 – Confirming the rebalance to proceed

> **Note**
> You must pay attention to the preceding dialog as it tells you that the SOBR will get put into Maintenance Mode for the duration of the rebalance operation. Proceed with caution!

After you click **Yes**, the rebalance operation will commence, and you will see the progress dialog come up:

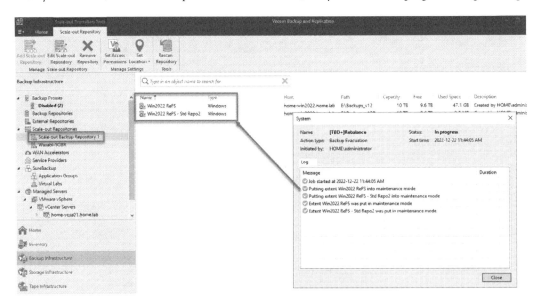

Figure 3.16 – SOBR Rebalance progress window

At this point, the only thing to do is wait for the rebalance to complete. Once it has been completed, you will be presented with a summary. Nothing may need to be rebalanced, but if data was rebalanced, details of how much will be displayed:

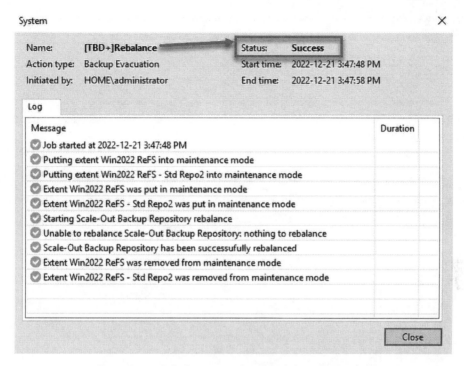

Figure 3.17 – Rebalance completed and showing success

In the previous screenshot, we didn't need to rebalance the SOBR. So, the summary window shows **Success**, and the details show nothing to rebalance.

When it comes to the SOBR Rebalance feature, there are some considerations and limitations you must take into account:

- If your SOBR contains only Object Storage extents, the **Rebalance** option won't be supported – it will not run.

- The **Rebalance** feature only works with available and non-archive repositories – it does not use the Capacity or Archive tiers.

- The minimum number of extents required is two.

- Unlike many other features that provide a wizard dialog, the rebalance feature does not – it will only show the progress dialog, as shown in *Figure 3.17*.

- All extents stay in Maintenance Mode during the process, and the SOBR is out of operation until it's finished.

- The amount of time taken for the rebalancing is based on the size of data to get moved around – the timing is typically unpredictable.

Other considerations and limitations can be found in the link in the *Further reading* section at the end of this chapter.

Exporting backups

Another feature added to Veeam Backup & Replication v12 is exporting backups from repositories, including a SOBR. This feature will synthesize or create a complete and independent full backup file (VBK) from the selected restore points located in your backup repositories. See the *Further reading* section for more information on the export feature.

To do this, use the **Export Backup** button located in the toolbar when on the **Home** tab:

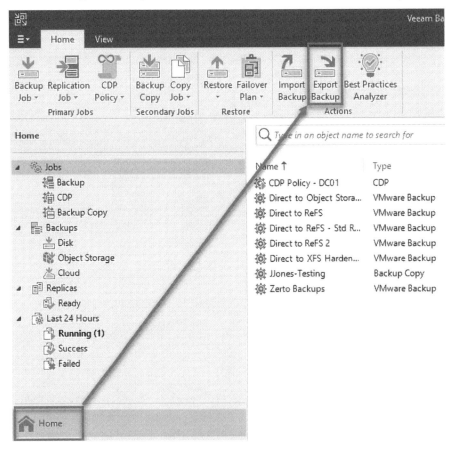

Figure 3.18 – Export Backup button

Once you have clicked the **Export Backup** button, you will be presented with the **Export Backup** dialog, where you either search for or use the **Add** button to select the backups to export:

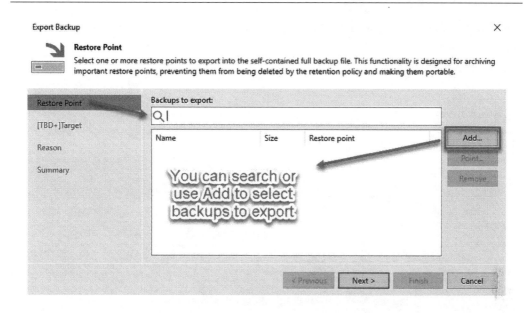

Figure 3.19 – Export Backup dialog to add backups for exporting

When you click the **Add** button, you will see all your backup jobs. Here, you can expand them to select the backup job you want to export, choose the server contained within that backup, and click **Add**:

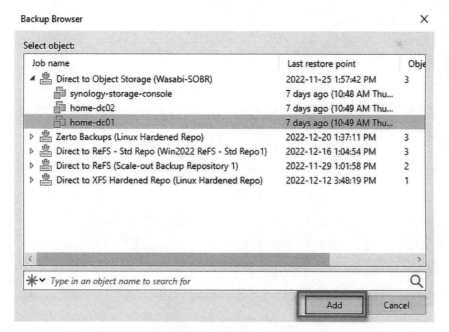

Figure 3.20 – Using Backup Browser to select a backup to export

When you are back at the **Export Backup** window after selecting the server to be restored, you can click the **Point** button to choose the restore point you wish to export if the latest one isn't selected:

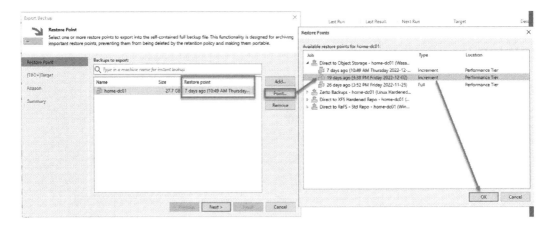

Figure 3.21 – Selecting a different restore point to export

After selecting a backup point and clicking **Next**, you will be able to select a **Backup repository** or **Local/Shared folder** option for your **Target**. You will also have the option to delete the exported backups automatically after *X* amount of time:

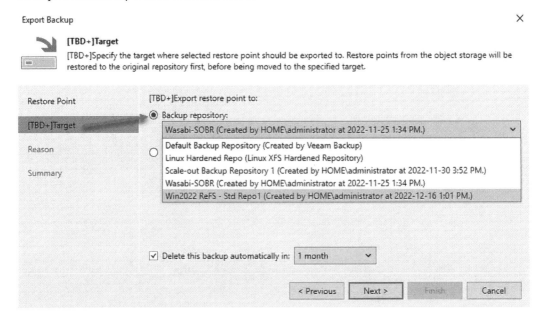

Figure 3.22 – Target selection to the backup repository

If you select **Local or shared folder**, you will have the option to choose a location on your local server drives:

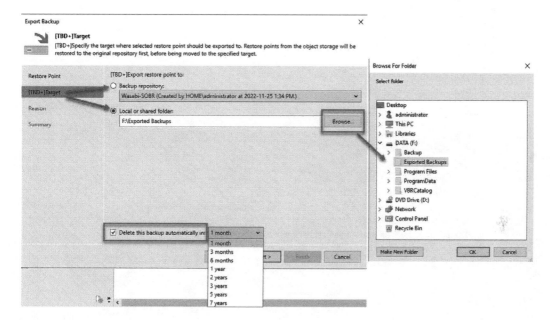

Figure 3.23 – Local or shared folder selection with Delete this backup automatically in: selected

After selecting your target, click **Next** and provide a reason for the restoration (this page can be hidden with a checkbox). Click **Next** to see the **Summary** screen, then click **Finish** to complete the export. You will then see a progress window to show the export of your restoration point:

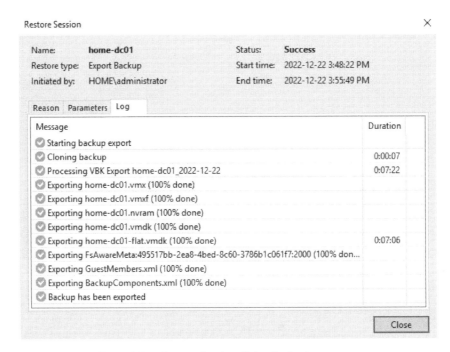

Figure 3.24 – Restore Session dialog for backup export

You will then see your export in the repository you chose. If you selected the local folder, as I did for this example, you will see the exported backup file on disk:

Figure 3.25 – Exported backup files to the local folder

The exported backup will also appear in the console under the **Backups | Disk (Exported)** section of the tree:

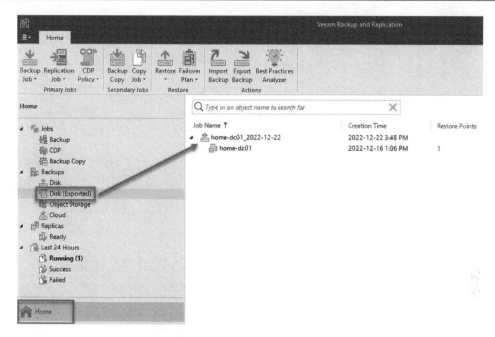

Figure 3.26 – Exported backup in the console for viewing

With that, we have looked at the last feature in this chapter on SOBR Rebalance and exporting.

Summary

This chapter reviewed SOBRs and some of the newest enhancements within Veeam Backup & Replication v12. We covered what is new with SOBR and direct-to-object storage for the performance tier. We also looked at VeeaMover and what it is, including its use cases. Finally, we looked at the SOBR Rebalance feature, which helps with data distribution between extents, and backing up exports to another repository or local/shared folder.

Hopefully, you will have gained a better understanding of some of the latest features to be added to the SOBR. The next chapter, *Tape Server and Other Enhancements*, will dive deep into the newest tape server role enhancements.

Further reading

To learn more about the topics that were covered in this chapter, take a look at the following resources:

- *SOBR Rebalance and Considerations and Limitations*: `https://helpcenter.veeam.com/docs/backup/vsphere/sobr_rebalance.html?ver=120`

- *Exporting Backups*: `https://helpcenter.veeam.com/docs/backup/vsphere/exporting_backups.html?ver=120`

4

Tape Servers and Other Enhancements

This chapter will look at tape servers and other enhancements to **Veeam Backup & Replication** (**VBR**) v12. We will look at having a tape server role with a Linux-based server and also at sending backups from object storage to tape. We will also look at **network attached storage** (**NAS**) backup direct to tape and better LTO9 support. Finally, we will look at other changes such as restoring "permissions only" for files, exporting **virtual machine** (**VM**) disks to another hypervisor, and the enhancements to the VM exclusions, which now include exclusion from everywhere!

By the end of this chapter, you will know about the changes to the tape server role, which includes a Linux-based server, NAS backup to tape and improved LTO9 support, and the other enhancements introduced to VBR v12.

In this chapter, we will cover the following main topics:

- Understanding what is new with tape servers and object storage to tape

- Learning about NAS backup to tape and improved LTO9 support

- Discovering other enhancements such as permissions, exporting, and exclusions

Technical requirements

For this chapter, a prior installation of VBR v12 will be required, as well as a Linux server to install the tape server role. *Chapter 1, Installation – Best Practices and Optimizations*, covered how to install/upgrade VBR, which you will leverage in this chapter. You can also reference the *Tape Devices Support* section of the Veeam website here:

```
https://helpcenter.veeam.com/docs/backup/vsphere/tape_device_support.
html?ver=120
```

Understanding what is new with tape servers and object storage to tape

Tape server support has evolved with VBR but has improved in v12 with the ability to support Linux as a tape server. One of the many reasons for allowing backup administrators to switch the tape server component over to Linux is the license cost savings from dispensing with a Microsoft Windows server. Previous to VBR v12, the tape server role could only be installed on a Microsoft Windows server, but now we have Linux as an option. You can read about the requirements for tape servers for supported Linux distributions and the supported tape hardware in the *Further reading* section at the end of the chapter.

For my examples in this book section, I will use a VM with CentOS 7.x installed and **Quadstor Virtual Tape Library (VTL)** software for Linux. Information about Quadstor VTL can be found here: `https://www.quadstor.com/virtual-tape-library.html`.

Using Linux for a tape server

To set up the Linux server as a tape server, we will need to add it from the **Tape Infrastructure** tab within the VBR v12 console, as shown in the following screenshot:

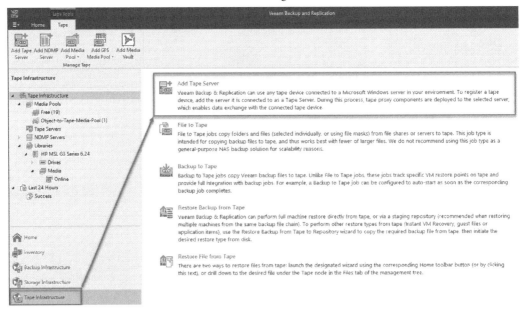

Figure 4.1 – The Tape Infrastructure tab with the Add Tape Server option

Click on the **Add Tape Server** option on the right side of the console window or use the **Add Tape Server** button in the toolbar:

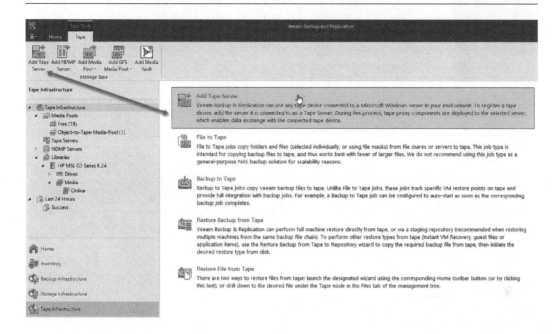

Figure 4.2 – The Add Tape Server options

When the **Add Tape Server** wizard opens, you are presented initially with your backup server in the drop-down list, but you can click the **Add New…** button and then select **Linux** to add your Linux tape server:

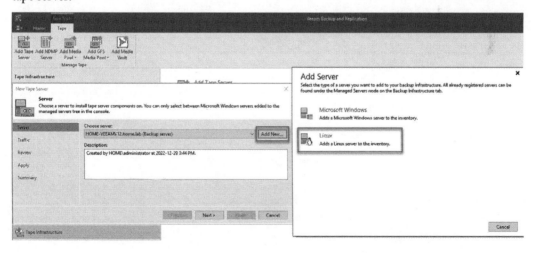

Figure 4.3 – The Add Tape Server wizard and the Add New… button for adding a Linux server

You will proceed through the **Linux** server wizard, adding the DNS name or IP address of your server along with the credentials for connectivity. Once completed, you will return to the **Add Tape Server** wizard with your new Linux server selected:

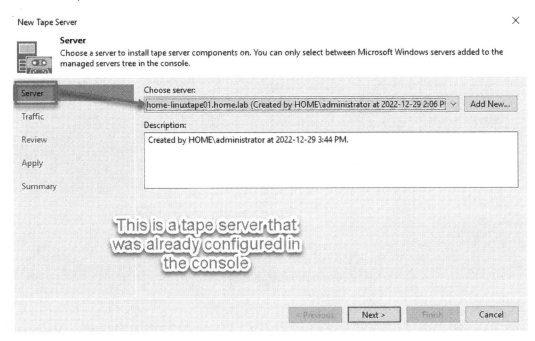

Figure 4.4 – Linux tape server selected after being added

Proceed through each tab of the wizard, modifying anything as needed. Once you get to the **Review** screen, ensure everything looks as it should:

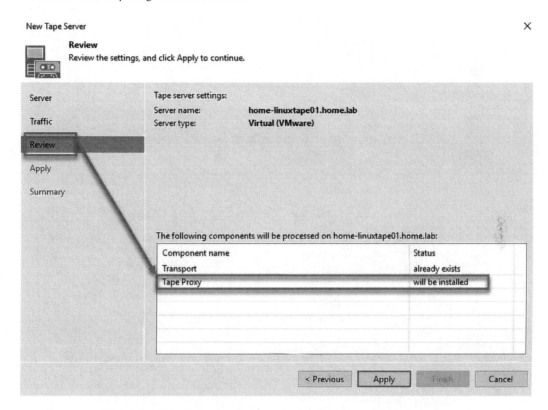

Figure 4.5 – The Review screen showing the Tape Proxy role installation

Click **Apply**. Once the process is completed, which includes loading the tape server role to the Linux server, you will see the following screen:

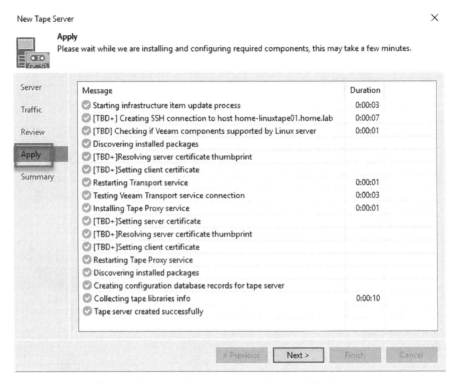

Figure 4.6 – The Apply screen showing the installation of the Tape Proxy service

After clicking **Next**, the **Summary** screen will appear:

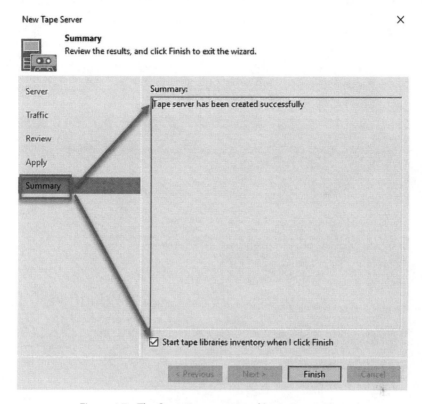

Figure 4.7 – The Summary screen and inventory option

> **Note**
> You will want to leave the **Start tape libraries inventory when I click Finish** option checked; this way, after the server is added to the VBR console, it will run an inventory on all tapes in the system.

You have now added your Linux tape server to VBR v12 for use with your backup. You can see the tape server, libraries, drives, and tapes all from within the **Tape Infrastructure** section of the console:

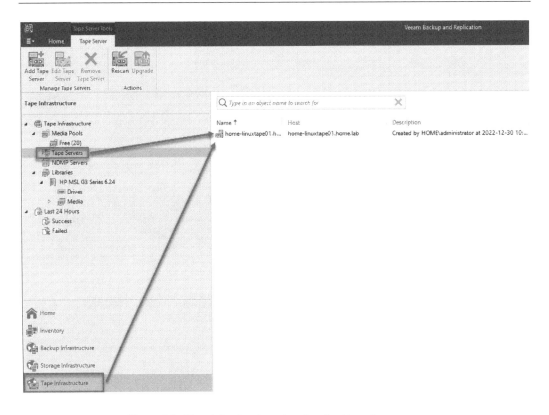

Figure 4.8 – Tape Infrastructure showing the Linux tape server

We have now covered using Linux for a tape server and how to add this to the VBR v12 console. Now, let's look at how we send backups direct from object storage to tape in VBR v12.

Object storage to tape

As discussed in previous chapters, with VBR v12, you can perform direct object storage backups, and now also the ability to perform object storage to tape. In previous versions, this was not possible, but with a repository made up of object storage, whether standard or **Scale-out Backup Repository** (**SOBR**), you can configure backup jobs to tape now that will send the backup data from these repositories or backup jobs.

You can have your backups made to object storage and then have the object storage sent to tape. You are also able to restore from tape to your infrastructure or other repositories:

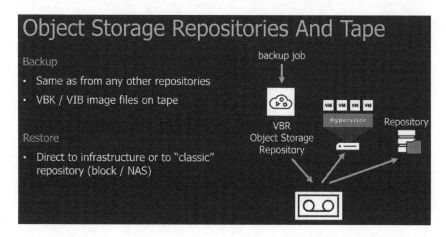

Figure 4.9 – Object to tape and restore to hypervisor or repository

To set up object storage to tape, you will need to create a new tape backup job using the toolbar or right-click menu:

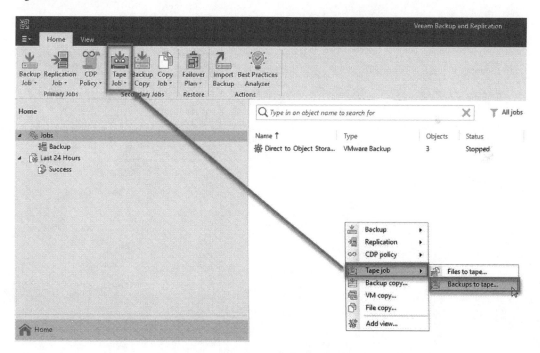

Figure 4.10 – New tape job for backups to tape

Once you start the **New Backup to Tape Job** wizard, you will be prompted for things such as the name of the job, backups, media pool, and more:

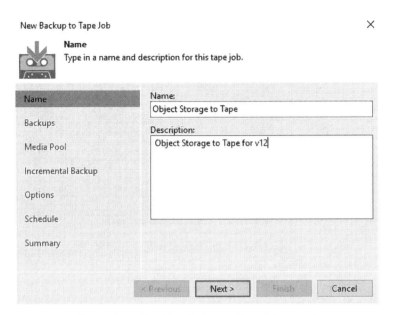

Figure 4.11 – The New Backup to Tape Job wizard

It is on the **Backups** tab of this wizard that the object storage to tape comes into play where you select either the repository, which is object storage, or a job that uses object storage as a repository:

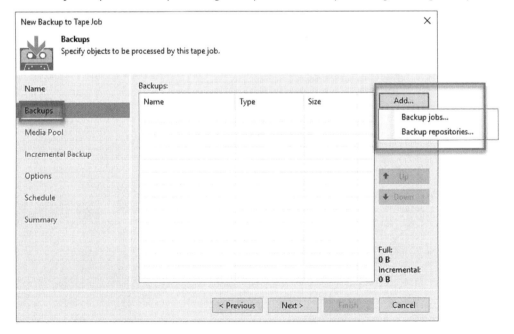

Figure 4.12 – Backup choice for job or repository to tape

The main options here are as follows:

- **Backup jobs…**: This allows the selection of backup jobs that you have configured to go to either a standard or SOBR backed by object storage

- **Backup repositories…**: This allows the selection of the backup repository, either standard or SOBR backed by object storage, to go directly to tape

Once you choose either the backup jobs or repositories added to the tape job, you then proceed through the remaining part of the wizard:

- **Media Pool**: Here, you choose a media pool (or create a new one) to use with the backup job to send data to tape:

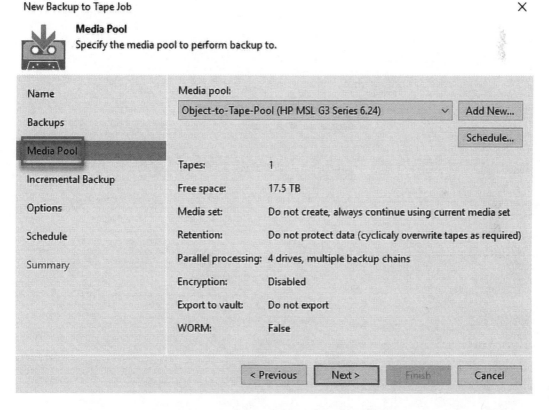

Figure 4.13 – The Media Pool selection and options

- **Incremental Backup**: This is where you select whether you want incremental backups to also go to tape or not; if not specified, then full backups will go to the tape:

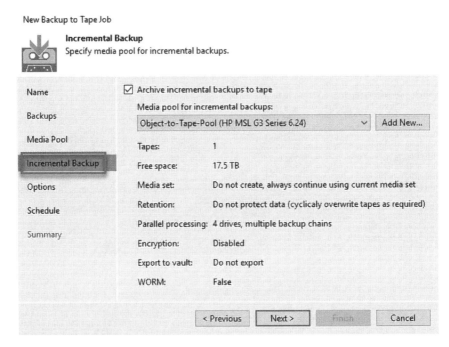

Figure 4.14 – Incremental backup options to send to tape

- **Options**: This is where you can select things such as ejecting the tape upon completion of the job, exporting the media set when the job completes, how many tape drives the job can use, and advanced options such as processing the latest full backup chain only:

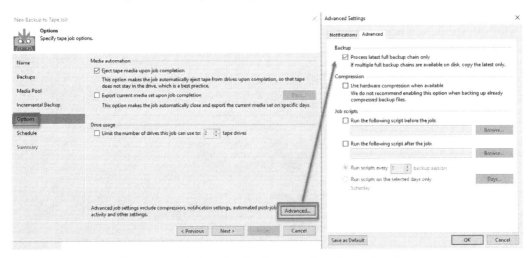

Figure 4.15 – Options for ejecting tape plus advanced settings

- **Schedule**: Here, you set up the schedule of when the job should run, which you can run right after your backup job if you choose to use **Backup** for the source. You can also enable a feature to prevent this job from being interrupted by source backup jobs to ensure that if it runs longer than usual, the primary backup job linked to it will not start until the tape job finishes:

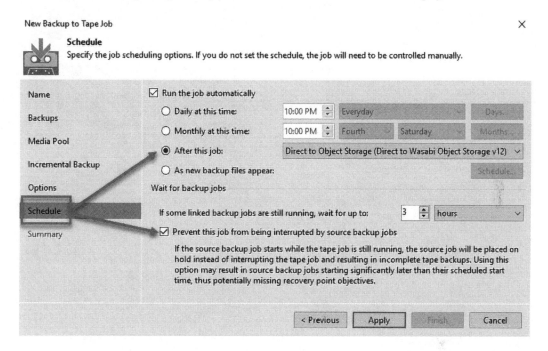

Figure 4.16 – Scheduling after the primary job and the interruption setting

- **Summary**: This shows the summary of your tape job and where you click **Finish** to create the job:

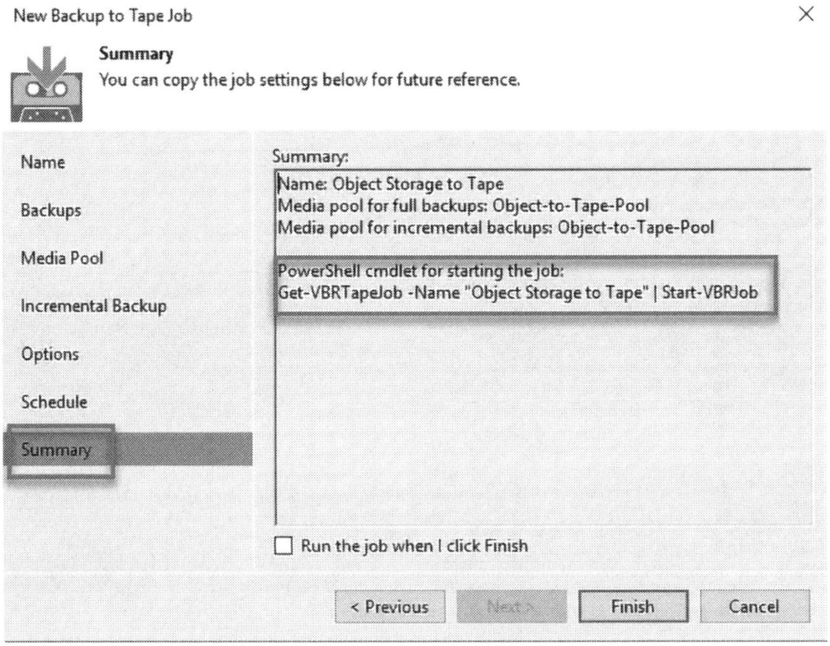

Figure 4.17 – Summary of backup to tape job

> **Note**
> In most summary screens, you will see that VBR provides PowerShell commands to configure or start a job, which can be beneficial for automation, amongst other things.

We have now covered what is new with tape servers, including using Linux for the tape server role, and we looked at the new object storage to tape feature, which can use backup jobs or repositories to offload data to tape. We will now look at doing NAS backup to tape and other enhancements.

NAS backup to tape and improved LTO9 support

Another significant enhancement to the backup-to-tape options is doing NAS backups to tape! Previously you could run a NAS backup to repositories, but the tape was unavailable in VBR v11. Now, with VBR v12, you can send NAS backups to tape and, similarly, send NAS backups to object storage.

The process for working with NAS backups to tape is the same as the previous *Object storage to tape* section. You create a backup to tape job using a media pool, but rather than choosing a backup job based on object storage, you select your NAS backup job as the source to send to the tape:

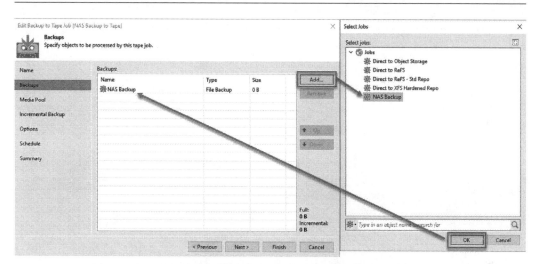

Figure 4.18 – Selecting NAS Backup to go to tape

The remaining screens in the **Backup to Tape Job** dialog noted in the previous screenshot are the same as the *Object storage to tape* section, which you can reference for further information.

Something else to mention when it comes to tape backups is looking at things outside your backups and VBR v12. Some of those things are set out in the following list:

- **Physical versus virtual tape**: When looking into your tape infrastructure, you must decide whether you use a physical tape unit or go **virtual tape library** (**VTL**). Some of this will depend on what you have in your infrastructure, as a physical tape library may require a direct connection to a server or switch, in the case of a fibre channel or **Internet Small Computer System Interface** (**iSCSI**). In contrast, a VTL can be installed on an existing virtual infrastructure if that is what you use – an example is VMware. Choose what best suits your environment, as both have pros and cons.

- **Storage (LTR)**: You need to plan your LTR storage requirements as this might require the purchase of many physical tapes for a physical library or, in the case of VTL, more storage. Once you have chosen your technology, you need to look at this as the next step.

- **Service-level agreement (SLA)**: When it comes to tape and using it for LTR, the restore times can be longer than restoring from fast disk storage, so you need to ensure you define your SLA requirements when a restore needs to be done from tape. In the case of the physical option, you might need to recall a tape from a vault, load it into the library, and then conduct the restore, which will take time. The same can be said for VTL if that is also set to vault tapes, as there is a recall process, loading, and restoring. Make sure you consider this, along with the other things mentioned here.

Regarding the new LTO9 support, the resolved issue in a VBR v11a patch is in v12, along with behind-the-scenes enhancements. The following link provides a reference to the v11a patch: `https://www.veeam.com/kb4245`.

We have now covered NAS backup to tape, including some other aspects when setting up your tape environment. Now, let's look at the final section of this chapter, which is about other enhancements made to VBR v12.

Other enhancements – permissions, exporting, and exclusions

VBR v12 has also introduced further enhancements to help backup administrators with day-to-day management tasks. Some of these new changes are as follows:

- **Permissions restore**: Typically, when you do file/folder level restores within VBR v12, it will restore both the folder/files and permissions. But what if you don't need to restore files/folders but rather fix the permissions on a folder/files or directory structure? Well, that is one of the changes made in v12, where you can restore just the file/folder permissions.

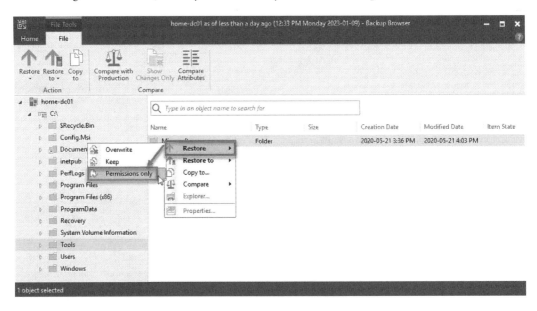

Figure 4.19 – File or folder permission restore option

- **VM exclusions**: You can now exclude a VM from being processed, excluding it from a job even when added to a backup job, a policy, or as part of a container, as noted.

Select **VM Exclusions** from the menu:

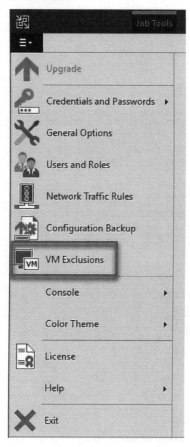

Figure 4.20 – The VM Exclusions option in the menu

Then click the **Add** button to select which VMs you want to be excluded:

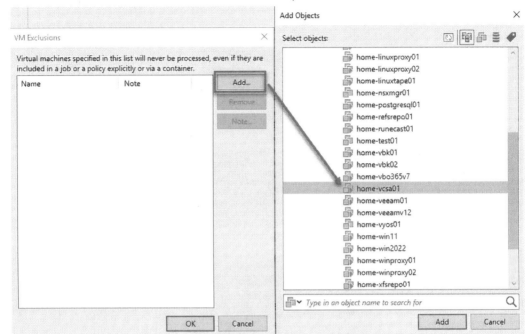

Figure 4.21 – Adding VMs to the exclusion list

> **Note**
>
> In the **VM Exclusions** list, note that when adding a virtual machine, it will then be excluded from processing whether included in a job, through a policy, or in a container.

- **Exporting to another hypervisor**: You can now export a VM backup to another hypervisor format. For example, you backed up a VM from VMware vSphere and want to export it to Microsoft Hyper-V to test. You can export the entire VM or just one of the VM disk files.

Follow these steps to export a VM as a virtual disk:

1. Click on the **Home** tab, select the **Disk** option under **Backups**, and expand the job for the VM you want to export. Right-click and select **Export content as virtual disks…**:

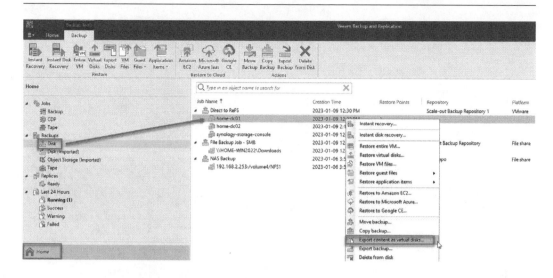

Figure 4.22 – The Export content as virtual disks option

2. The **Export Disk** wizard pops up. Select the **Restore Point** option and click **Next >**:

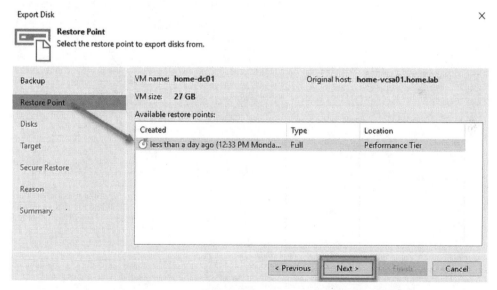

Figure 4.23 – Selecting the Restore Point option to export

3. After clicking **Next**, you are presented with the **Disks** screen to select the specific VM disks to export:

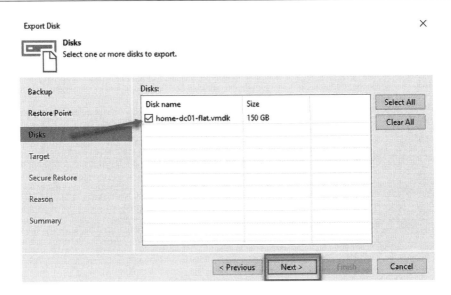

Figure 4.24 – Selecting the required disks for the VM

4.   After you select the needed disks, click **Next**. You then will be shown the **Target** screen where you can choose different hypervisor formats, which include **VMDK** (**VMware vSphere**) and **VHD** or **VHDX**, which are the **Microsoft Hyper-V** formats:

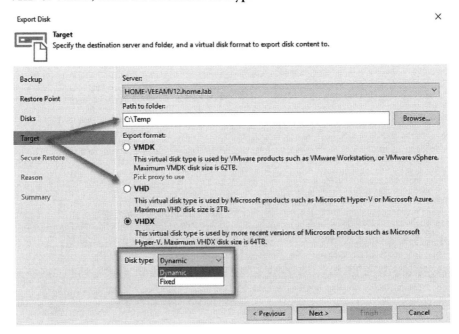

Figure 4.25 – Selecting a folder and destination format of the exported disk(s)

> **Note**
>
> When you select one of the Microsoft Hyper-V formats – **VHD** or **VHDX**, you can choose whether the disk will be **Dynamic** or **Fixed**. **Dynamic** is a disk created based on the used size of the disk within VMware, and **Fixed** is a disk created for the actual size of the provisioned disk in VMware.

5.   After you have made your selection, click **Next**. You will be prompted to select a **Secure Restore** option, where you can have your exported disks scanned by your antivirus vendor to ensure there are no infections. This is an optional step (it can be bypassed by unchecking the box):

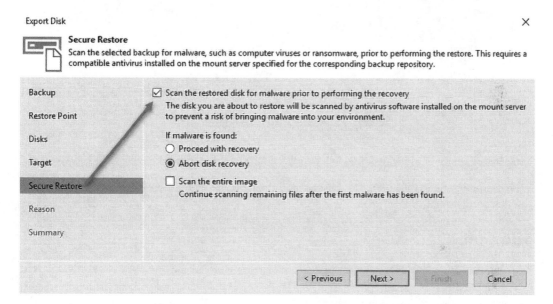

Figure 4.26 – Secure Restore selection if required

6.   After choosing the **Secure Restore** settings and clicking **Next**, you get asked to define the reason for the restore, which is optional. Click **Next** to review the **Summary** page. Click on **Finish** to begin the export process:

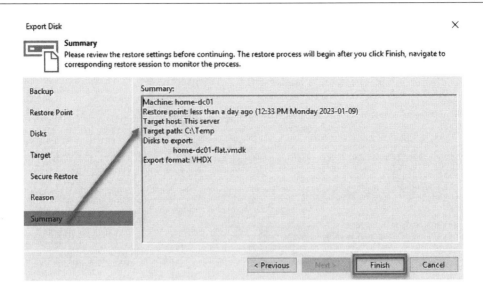

Figure 4.27 – Summary of disk export

Your export begins, and the disk files will be placed in the folder selected during the export wizard.

We have now come to the end of this chapter and the newest enhancements for VBR v12. Let's now summarize the chapter.

Summary

This chapter has reviewed the tape server, including using Linux as the operating system. We looked at adding a Linux server to the Veeam console so that the tape server role can be installed. We also looked at how you can send from object storage repositories to tape directly from the repository or via a backup job. We covered how you can now send NAS backups to tape for archiving purposes and enhanced LTO9 support. Then, we learned about some of the newest enhancements to VBR v12, including restoring file/folder permissions, VM exclusions, and exporting disks to other hypervisor formats.

Hopefully, you now have a better understanding of the tape server role and other enhancements for sending data to tape. The next chapter will look at the enhanced security measures within VBR v12.

Further reading

To learn more about the topics that got covered in this chapter, take a look at the following resources:

- Tape server operating system requirements including Linux: `https://helpcenter.veeam.com/docs/backup/vsphere/system_requirements.html?ver=120#tape-server`

- Supported tape hardware: `https://helpcenter.veeam.com/docs/backup/vsphere/system_requirements.html?ver=120#tape`

Part 2: Security, Object Storage Direct, CDP, and Cloud Connect

This section aims to cover the newest features of Veeam Backup & Replication v12. You will learn about the **Continuous Data Protection (CDP)** feature of v12 and about using it with Veeam Cloud Connect. You will also learn about the new security enhancement within the console. We will discuss the new object storage enhancements including Direct to Object storage for repositories. We also look at the NAS backup and all of the changes made. By the end of this section, you will have a wealth of knowledge on new features to implement and use in your environments.

The following chapters are included in this section:

- *Chapter 5, Veeam's New Enhanced Security Features*
- *Chapter 6, Object Storage – What's New and Enhancements*
- *Chapter 7, What's New in NAS Backup*
- *Chapter 8, CDP and Veeam Cloud Connect*

5

Veeam's New Enhanced Security Features

Veeam Backup & Replication (**VBR**) v12 has some significant new enhancements to the security aspect of the application. This chapter will look at some of the more critical changes. The first thing discussed will be the improvements to using **multi-factor authentication** (**MFA**) for console login and **group-managed service account** (**gMSA**) support. You will learn how Linux no longer requires **Secure Shell** (**SSH**) or **super user do** (**SUDO**) for management. Lastly, we will look at the auto-logoff feature for the console allowing resources to be kept in check.

By the end of this chapter, you will understand what is new in security for version v12 and also how to leverage these new enhancements. Finally, you will gain a better understanding of how the overall changes implemented help secure your backup environment.

We will cover the following main topics in this chapter:

- Understanding MFA and gMSA support

- Understanding Linux – SSH or SUDO are not required

- Discovering the new auto-logoff feature

Technical requirements

For this chapter, you should have VBR v12 installed. If you have followed along through the book, *Chapter 1, Installation – Best Practices and Optimizations,* covered the installation and upgrading of VBR, which you can leverage in this chapter.

Understanding MFA and gMSA support

When installing the latest VBR v12, security focuses on the console to ensure secure access. Previously, you were required to be a local administrator on the VBR server to run the console. Now, you can add users with MFA. So, what is MFA, or what does MFA do? It is an added layer of security that utilizes a "code" you are required to input on top of your login credentials to be able to access the console for logging in. You can use one of the many MFA applications available out there, such as the following:

- Google Authenticator

- Microsoft Authenticator

- Authy

Turning on MFA forces the user logging in to the VBR console to input both their login credentials, consisting of a username and password, and the MFA code generated by their chosen application. If they do not use the MFA code, then login is denied to the console, giving you that extra layer of security.

To turn on MFA for user accounts, you do the following:

1. Open the VBR console, click on the hamburger menu, and select **Users and Roles**:

Figure 5.1 – Selecting the Users and Roles option for MFA

2. You are presented with a **Security** dialog where you can add users and enable MFA:

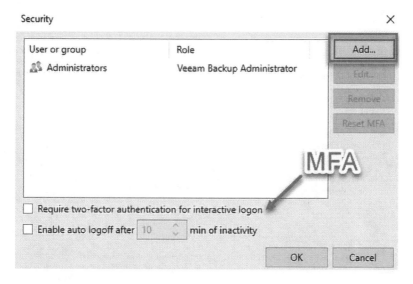

Figure 5.2 – The Security dialog where you can add and enable MFA

3. Use the **Add** button to add your local user and then turn on MFA by checking the **Require two-factor authentication for interactive logon** box:

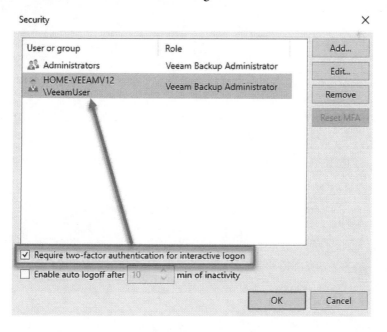

Figure 5.3 – Selecting the user and turning MFA on

4. Click **OK** to close the dialog, and now we can log on as **VeeamUser** to the console to enable MFA.

> **Note**
>
> If a Security group is added to the **Security** window, you will receive a message about removing the group and only adding users to allow MFA.

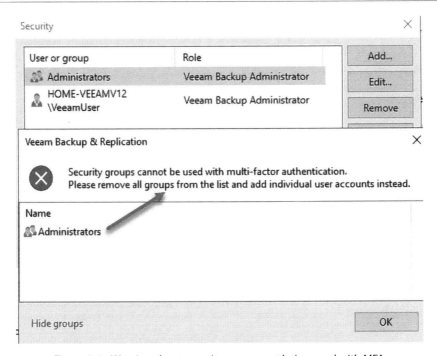

Figure 5.4 – Warning about security groups not being used with MFA

5. Remove the required security group, add the required users to this dialog, and proceed to the next step.

6. Launch the console from the desktop icon, enter the credentials for the user added to the **Security** dialog, and click **Connect**:

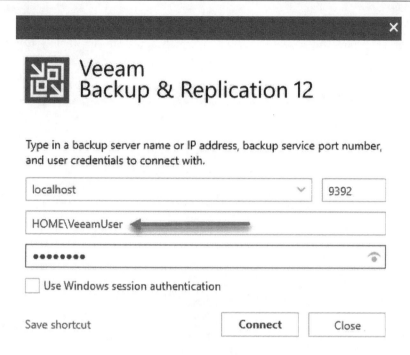

Figure 5.5 – User credentials added to the Security section

7. Once you click **Connect**, you will be prompted to set up MFA using one of your chosen applications. In my example, I will use **Authy** to configure MFA for **VeeamUser**:

Figure 5.6 – MFA prompt to set it up for the user

8. Scan the QR code or enter the manual code into your authentication application. Click **Next** to proceed. You will be presented with a **Confirmation code** dialog where you enter the code from your authentication application:

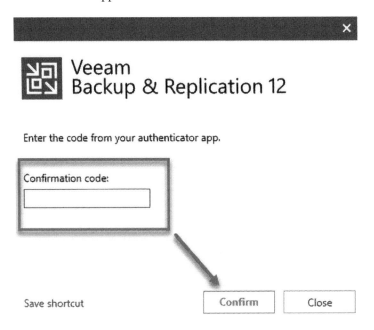

Figure 5.7 – Confirmation code from the authentication application

9. After you enter the correct code in the required box and click **Confirm**, the console will open for the user.

> **Note**
>
> When you turn on MFA, it applies to all users within the list under **Security**, as shown in the preceding steps. Therefore, if you need to have a user excluded from MFA, then you need to have MFA turned off for all, which in the end, degrades your security.

Additional MFA settings

There are some other things you can do with MFA to ensure even further security, and these are listed as follows:

*   **MFA within a guest operating system (OS)**: Most guest OSes support some form of MFA login to go along with using your password. Some options include using an authenticator application, a security key, a face ID, and a PIN. While all of these are secure, using an authenticator application or security key is considered more secure.

- **MFA Offline**: Setting up MFA also works when your system is offline, meaning not on the domain but in a workgroup or not connected to the network. This option is helpful for air gaps with backups and your infrastructure.

Another great security feature added to VBR v12 is gMSA. What are gMSA accounts, you might ask? Well, gMSA has all the features of a **standalone managed service account (sMSA)** but extends functionality over multiple servers. Please see the *Further reading* section for more information. Some of the features are as follows:

- Automatic password management
- Simplified **service principal name (SPN)** management
- Delegation of management to other administrators
- Ability to get used across multiple servers

The gMSA is used in conjunction with the Microsoft Key Distribution Service, which keeps a secret key identifier that is used with the gMSA account. It is essential for the practical application use of gMSA accounts, allowing administrators to not worry about password synchronization with your services as it is all auto-managed from the domain controllers.

Benefits of using gMSAs

Using a gMSA offers users a single identity solution with enhanced security and helps reduce administrative overhead. It provides the following benefits:

- **Strong passwords**: A gMSA uses 240-byte randomly generated complex passwords. Using a complicated and lengthy password helps to minimize the chances of a service being brute-forced or a dictionary attack.
- **Cycling of passwords**: The gMSA password is managed by the Windows OS and is changed every 30 days (this can be modified when creating the gMSA account). With this, administrators are no longer required to schedule changing the password or managing service outages, which helps to keep service accounts secure.
- **Support for simplified SPN management**: When setting up a gMSA account via PowerShell, you set the SPN during account creation, allowing services to support automatic SPN registration against the gMSA account.

The preceding section was a brief explanation of what gMSA accounts are used for and their benefits, but to learn more, please check out the link in the *Further reading* section at the end of the chapter.

To add a gMSA account to the VBR console, complete the following steps:

1. From the hamburger menu, select **Credentials and Passwords**, then **Datacenter Credentials**:

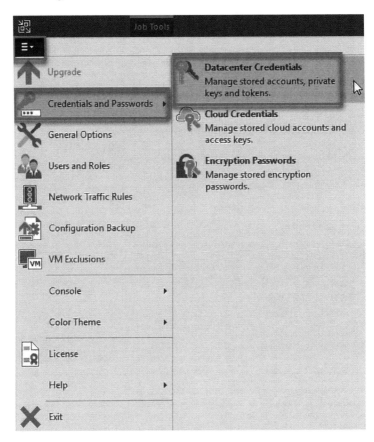

Figure 5.8 – Datacenter Credentials to add a gMSA account

2. The **Manage Credentials** window now opens. Click **Add...** and then select **Managed service account...**:

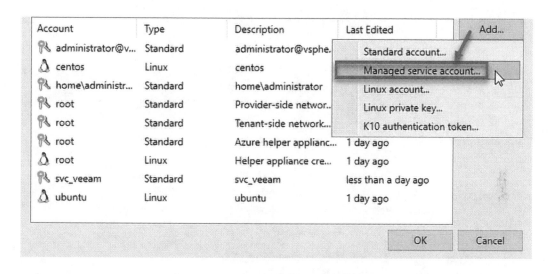

Figure 5.9 – Managed service account… selection

3. You will then type in the domain account, the gMSA account:

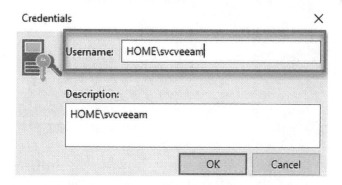

Figure 5.10 – Username for the gMSA account

4. Type a value in the **Username** field and click **OK** to proceed to add the gMSA account. You will then see the account in the credentials list displayed as **Managed service account**:

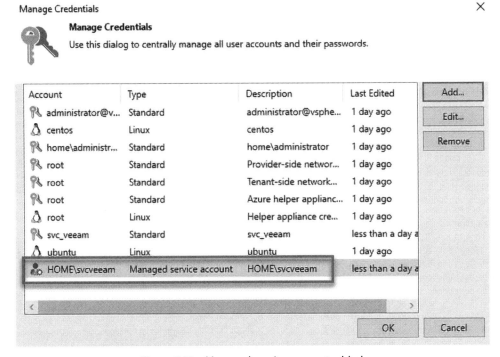

Figure 5.11 – Managed service account added

This process now completes the process for adding a gMSA account to the VBR console to be used within the environment.

> **Note**
> When added, the account shows a different icon to signify that it is a managed service account from the domain. Domain accounts are the only supported ones for gMSA, and you cannot use servers not part of an Active Directory domain.

We have completed the new MFA and gMSA account features section within VBR v12. Now, let us look at something else that is changing: Linux connectivity not requiring SSH or SUDO.

Understanding Linux – SSH or SUDO are not required

Using a Linux server, you typically need some form of SSH or SUDO to connect and install components or make changes. In Veeam v11, you were required to have these services when working with Linux servers that had been added to VBR, except for hardened repositories.

With Linux hardened repositories, VBR v12 has made enhancements so that once you have added the repository to the system, you no longer need the single-use credential account in the SUDO group. In addition, you can further improve security by turning off SSH on the server.

So how does Veeam communicate with the Linux hardened repository if these things are disabled? Well, during the setup of the Linux hardened repository, the system creates a certificate, which is stored in the VBR database, and it is with this that further communication is handled. The certificate allows the following:

- Component upgrades, for example, the transport or installer services
- Modifying settings within the Linux hardened repository, for example, concurrent tasks
- Managing all aspects from within the Veeam environment

This section covered the changes to Linux hardened repositories with the requirement of SSH and SUDO being replaced by certificates within the database. Now, let's look at another feature to help with security and system resources on the VBR server.

Discovering the new Auto-Logoff feature

In prior VBR versions, when a user connected remotely to work via a **Remote Desktop Protocol** (**RDP**) session, many backup administrators would open the VBR console and then disconnect from their session. Disconnecting does a few things when it comes to both security and system resources:

- **Security**: It keeps the console open, so if an attacker gained access to an RDP session, they could easily then access your Veeam environment
- **System resources**: When you leave the console open and then you disconnect an RDP session, this keeps the memory used and does not release it, leading to high memory and CPU usage

So to combat this within VBR v12, a new enhancement called **auto logoff** has been added. What does auto logoff do, you might be asking? Well, it helps to address the issue covered in the preceding points, allowing for better security and freeing system resources on the VBR server.

To enable auto logoff, you must complete the following steps:

1.   Open the VBR v12 console.
2.   Click on the hamburger menu and select **Users and Roles** from the menu:

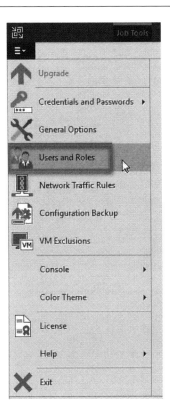

Figure 5.12 – Users and Roles selection

3. The **Security** dialog will open on the screen:

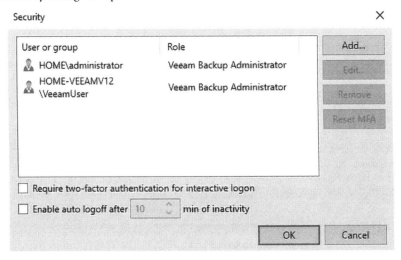

Figure 5.13 – The Security dialog

4. From within the **Security** dialog, check the **Enable auto logoff after X min of inactivity** checkbox to enable auto logoff:

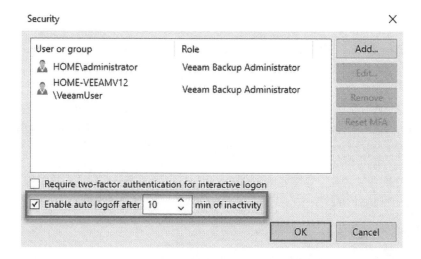

Figure 5.14 – The auto logoff feature enabled

5. Modify the number of minutes for which you want the system to wait before it logs a user off the VBR console.

6. Click the **OK** button to confirm the setting and close the dialog.

> **Note**
>
> When enabled, the default timing for the auto logoff feature is 10 minutes, but you can modify this to be shorter or longer based on your requirements. Keep in mind the longer the duration, the higher the security risk and system resource usage until the given time elapses.

We have now covered the last topic for this chapter regarding the auto logoff feature and how it can help with both securities and system resource usage.

This section looked at further enhancements within the VBR v12 system related to security and Linux hardened repository servers. We are now at the end of this chapter and will summarize all the topics covered.

Summary

This chapter reviewed many of the new security enhancements Veeam has added to v12. First, we examined using the MFA setting in the VBR console to enhance security and require a code for logging in to the console. Then, we looked at the Linux hardened repository enhancement, which does not require SSH or SUDO now and uses certificates to manage and update components. Lastly, we discussed the new auto logoff feature, which helps enhance security and free up system resources. After reading this chapter, you should better understand the multitude of new features added for the security of the VBR console and services.

Hopefully, you will understand how these improvements can better secure your environment. The next chapter will examine object storage enhancements and new third-party integrations with Microsoft Azure and Wasabi.

Further reading

Refer to the following resources for more information:

- gMSA overview (Microsoft): `https://learn.microsoft.com/en-us/windows-server/security/group-managed-service-accounts/group-managed-service-accounts-overview`

- gMSA accounts explanation and benefits (Azure): `https://learn.microsoft.com/en-us/azure/active-directory/fundamentals/service-accounts-group-managed`

- gMSA accounts (Veeam): `https://helpcenter.veeam.com/docs/backup/vsphere/using_gmsa.html?ver=120`

- MFA: `https://helpcenter.veeam.com/docs/backup/vsphere/mfa.html?ver=120`

6

Object Storage – What's New and Enhancements

Object storage is one of the many options for backup storage and repositories, and with **Veeam Backup & Replication** (**VBR**) v12, this is further enhanced. This chapter will look at new options for sending directly to object storage and using object storage in the **scale-out backup repository** (**SOBR**) performance tier. We will discuss how with **grandfather-father-son** (**GFS**) backup jobs, you can send to object storage with the immutability turned on now. Finally, we will look at enhancements to third-party integrations within the console for Microsoft Azure and Wasabi object storage.

By the end of this chapter, you will understand how to send backups directly to object storage, including within a SOBR. You will also understand how GFS can leverage object storage with immutability. Finally, you will better understand the new third-party application integrations into the console.

In this chapter, we will cover the following main topics:

- Understanding new direct-to-object storage and its use in SOBR
- Understanding GFS backups to object storage with immutability
- Discovering third-party integrations within the console for Azure and Wasabi

Technical requirements

If you have been following along from the start of the book, you will know that *Chapter 1, Installation – Best Practices and Optimizations*, covered the installation and optimization of VBR, which you can leverage in this chapter. For this chapter, you should have VBR installed. If you have access to object storage with a newer vendor, that would be an added benefit, but it is not required.

Understanding new direct-to-object storage and its use in SOBR

Before VBR v12, the only use case for object storage was using it as a capacity or archive tier within a SOBR. The release of VBR v12 changed this and allows users to scale their storage requirements much more easily and not have to manage capacity as much as using block storage.

Direct to object is a new feature introduced with VBR v12. It allows users to move away from block storage and send their data directly to object storage, on-premises, or in the cloud, with one of the many vendors such as Microsoft Azure, AWS, Wasabi, and so on. The feature allows you to use object storage in the performance tier of a SOBR, of which you can use multiple object storage extents, but the caveat is that they have to be from the same vendor. You cannot mix object and non-object storage, such as Microsoft Azure and AWS; both need to be from the same vendor to be a valid configuration.

> **Note**
> In the following examples on how to configure the direct-to-object storage for SOBR, I am using Wasabi as the object storage for my lab as I have an account with them. You can use whatever object storage you prefer, as many of them are compatible, including the big ones such as Microsoft Azure, Google Cloud, and AWS. You may also use on-premises object storage as well.

The following will outline how to set up the direct-to-object storage using a standard repository and a SOBR. We will go through the steps to add two Wasabi repositories and then configure them in a SOBR, and we will also add a third that will be a standard repository. To add a Wasabi object storage repository, do the following:

1. Click on the **Backup Infrastructure** tab and select **Backup Repositories**.

2. Right-click and select **Add backup repository...** or use the **Add Repository** button in the toolbar:

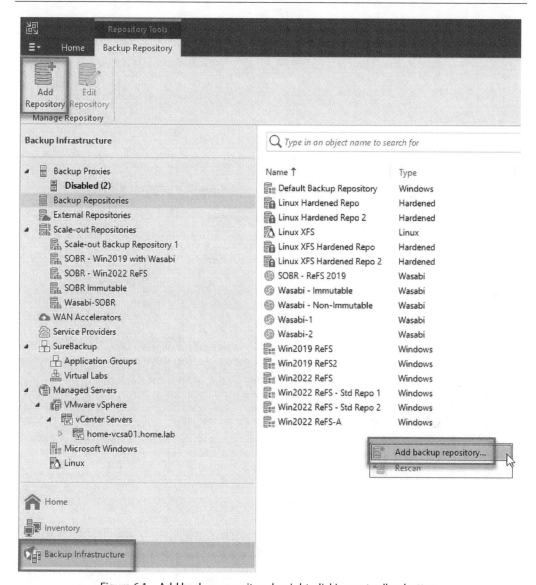

Figure 6.1 – Add backup repository by right-clicking or toolbar button

3. Click on **Object storage** in the **Add Backup Repository** dialog, as shown in *Figure 6.2*:

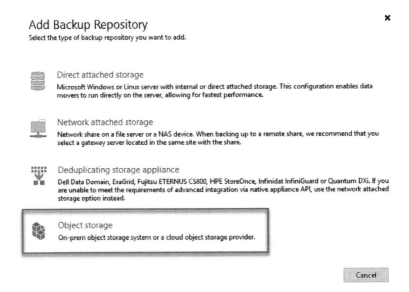

Figure 6.2 – Object storage selection

4.   After selecting **Object storage**, you can choose the vendor you will use for your object storage; in my case, I selected **Wasabi Cloud Storage**, as shown in *Figure 6.3*:

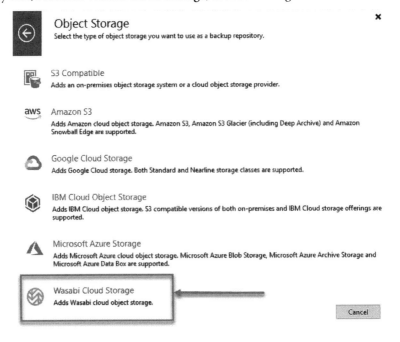

Figure 6.3 – Wasabi Cloud Storage as the Object Storage selection

5.   You are then presented with the **New Object storage Repository** dialog, where you provide the name of the repository, Wasabi-3, and enter a description, as shown in *Figure 6.4*:

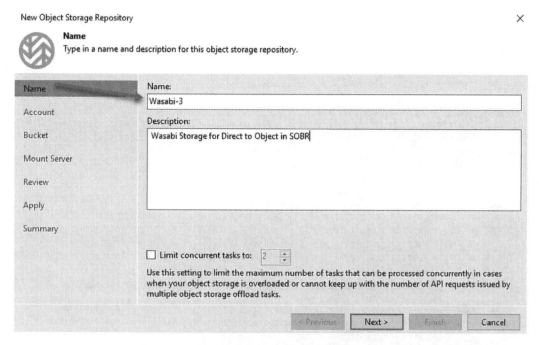

Figure 6.4 – The New Object Storage Repository dialog

6. Click the **Next >** button to continue to the **Account** page, where you will enter values for **Region**, **Credentials**, and **Connection Mode**:

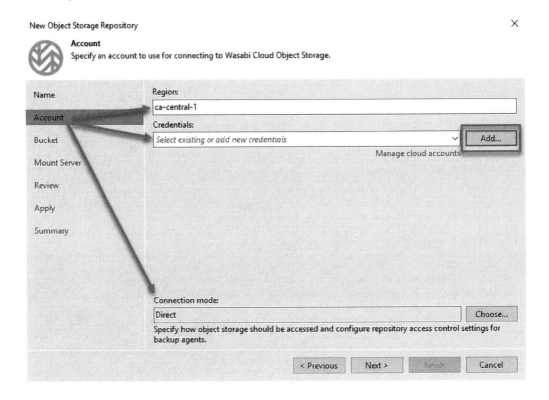

Figure 6.5 – The Account page with details and the Add… button to input credentials

> **Note**
>
> If this is a new installation, you may not have any saved credentials in the system, so you will need to use the **Add…** button to input your **Access Key** and **Secret Key** for connecting.

7. Click **Next >** to proceed to the **Bucket** page of the dialog, where you select the **Bucket** and **Folder** options to use for backups, as shown in *Figure 6.6*. You can use the **Browse…** buttons to select the bucket and the folder and create a new folder:

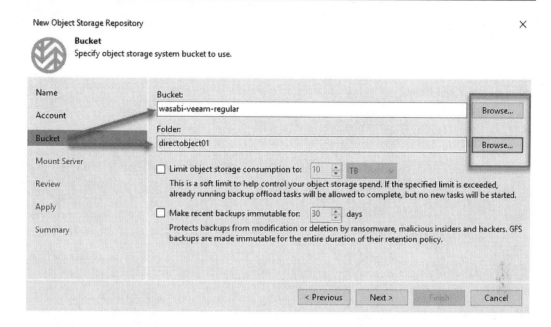

Figure 6.6 – Selecting the bucket and folder for object storage backups

8. Click **Next** > again to proceed to the **Mount Server** screen of the wizard where the backup server usually gets selected as the **Mount server** value, as shown in *Figure 6.7*:

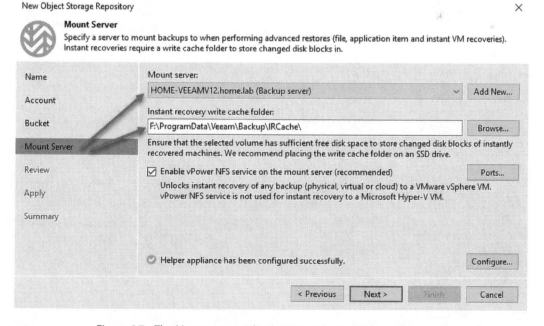

Figure 6.7 – The Mount server selection – usually the backup server itself

9. Click **Next** > again to proceed to the **Review** screen, which will highlight whether any components need to be installed. Once you've reviewed the components, click the **Apply** button to proceed, as shown in *Figure 6.8*:

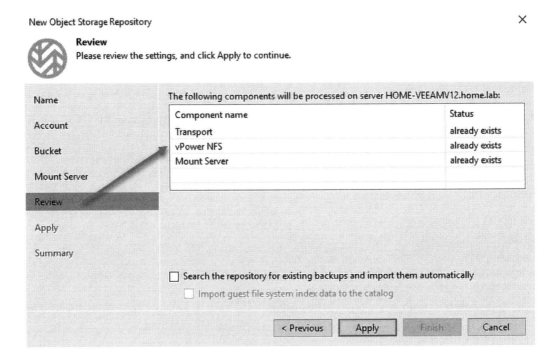

Figure 6.8 – Required components on the Review screen

10. You then will see the **Apply** screen in the wizard, which will install components if required or proceed through updating the database records:

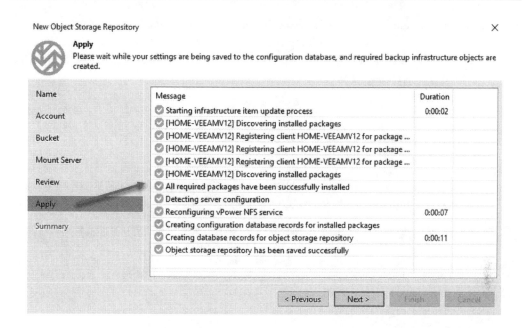

Figure 6.9 – The Apply screen installing components or updating the database

11. Click **Next >** to move to the **Summary** screen and **Finish** to complete the wizard, as shown in *Figure 6.10*:

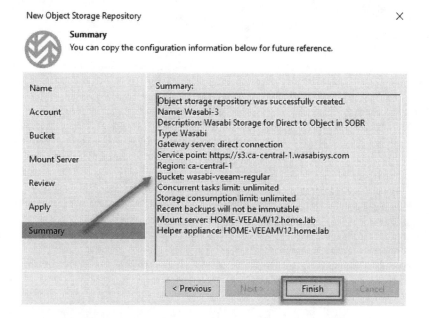

Figure 6.10 – The Summary screen showing the final setup steps

These steps complete adding a standard repository pointed to Wasabi object storage. To demonstrate the direct-to-object storage for a standard repository and SOBR, I have followed the preceding steps twice to create two more standard repositories: Wasabi-4 and Wasabi-5. They will be used in the SOBR repository as the performance extents.

The repositories that were created will be used as follows:

- **Wasabi-3**: A standard repository to send backup data

- **Wasabi-4/Wasabi-5**: SOBR to send backup data

In the following screenshot, you can see the standard backup repositories created for object storage, which will be used within the SOBR, shown in *Figure 6.12*:

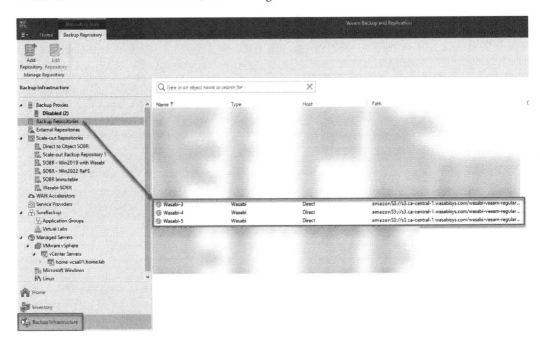

Figure 6.11 – Wasabi repositories used for direct-to-object storage

The **Wasabi-4/Wasabi-5** repositories were added to a SOBR, as in the following screenshot:

Figure 6.12 – SOBR for direct-to-object storage with Wasabi

Once you have configured either a standard repository or a SOBR for your backups, you need to create a backup job pointing to one of them. I have created two jobs, one directed to the standard repository (**Wasabi-3**) and one to SOBR (**Wasabi-4/Wasabi-5**) for this example.

A standard repository backup job

The following screenshot shows how a job is configured to point at a standard backup repository created from the preceding steps:

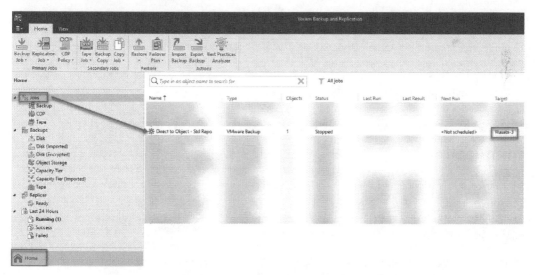

Figure 6.13 – Backup job to a standard direct-to-object storage repository

The next diagram will show the standard repositories created in the preceding steps, but this time the backup job is configured to point to the SOBR created from the repositories.

SOBR backup job

The following screenshot shows how a job is configured to point at a SOBR backup repository created from the preceding steps:

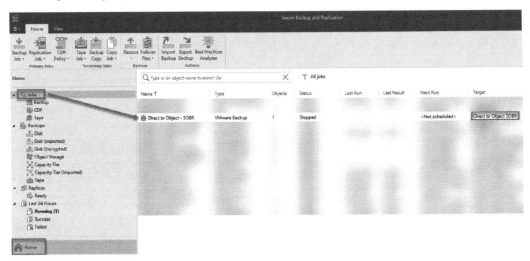

Figure 6.14 – Backup job to SOBR for a direct-to-object a repository

As you can see in the preceding screenshots, the jobs I created go to either the standard repository (**Wasabi-3**) or the SOBR (**Wasabi-4/Wasabi-5**). For my examples, these backups will send jobs directly to object storage in the chosen provider, in this case, Wasabi.

We have now covered the new direct-to-object storage for VBR v12. Now, let's look at using GFS backups to send to object storage using immutability.

Understanding GFS backups to object storage with immutability

Object storage with VBR v12 is intended for long-term data storage in the case of your GFS backups, but now it can also be used for short-term storage with performance extents in a SOBR. The repositories are either a cloud solution or an Amazon **Simple Storage Service** (**S3**)-compatible storage solution that can be on-premises.

To go along with the new direct-to-object storage backups, which can be used with immutable repositories, you can now set up backup copy jobs with GFS going to these same immutable repositories. So, what does this give you? Some of the benefits are presented in the following list:

- A second copy of your data to ensure you are meeting the *3-2-2-1-0 backup rule* for backups

- Another copy of your backups on immutable storage
- A second copy of data in another location or possibly a **disaster recovery** (DR) site

So, how do we set up GFS backups to be sent to immutable object storage? Using the processes already detailed in previous chapters, we can apply the following steps to configure a backup copy job with GFS retention to immutable object storage.

Configuring a backup copy job with GFS retention to immutable object storage

Complete these steps:

1. Open the VBR v12 console and navigate to the **Home** tab in the **Jobs** section in the tree. Right-click and select **Backup Copy…** or click on the **Backup Copy** button in the toolbar, as in *Figure 6.15*:

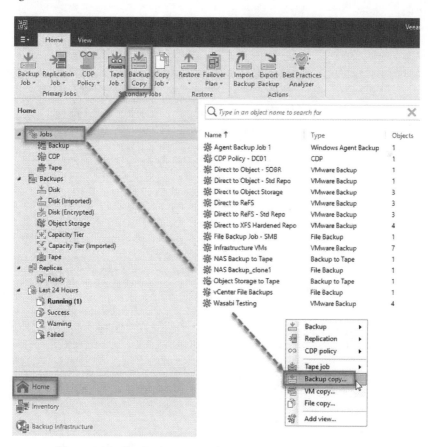

Figure 6.15 – The Backup copy job option to create a GFS backup

2.   You are then presented with the **New Backup Copy Job** dialog. Enter the **Name** and **Description** values, then select the **Copy mode** option, as shown in *Figure 6.16*:

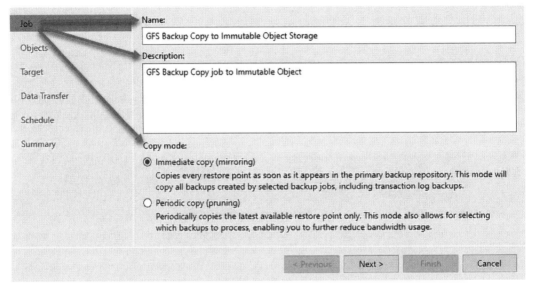

Figure 6.16 – The New Backup Copy Job dialog

> **Note**
>
> Be sure to read the **Copy mode** options to ensure you select the specific option you want to implement. Both do the same thing in the end, using different methods. More on this can be found in the *Further reading* section at the end of the chapter.

3. Click **Next >** to proceed to the **Objects** step, where you can select **From jobs…** or **From repositories…**, as shown in *Figure 6.17*:

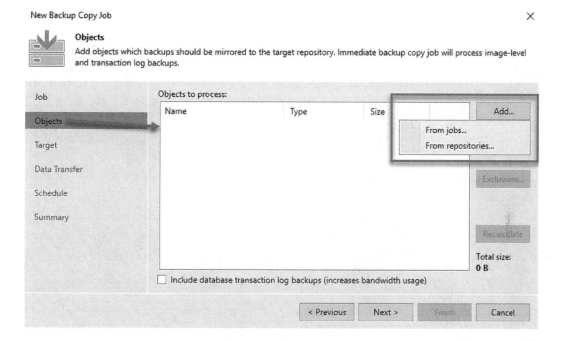

Figure 6.17 – Selecting Objects for a backup copy job

4. Click **Next >** to move to the **Target** tab in the dialog. Here, you will select the **Backup repository** option and turn on the **Keep certain full backups longer for archival purposes** GFS option. Click the **Configure** button to set the GFS options, as shown in the following screenshot. In my example, I will keep backups for two weeks and one month for my GFS retention:

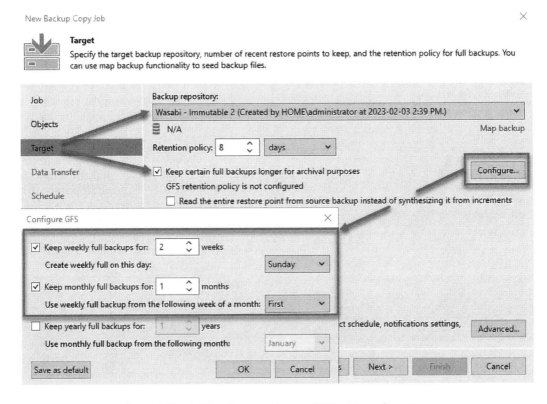

Figure 6.18 – Setting the repository and GFS with configuration

> **Note**
> The repository selected for the backup copy job is an immutable Wasabi repository to demonstrate sending to immutable object storage.

5. After clicking **Next >**, you will be in the **Data Transfer** section of the wizard. Here, you select **Direct** or **Through built-in WAN accelerators** to send the data, as shown in the following screenshot:

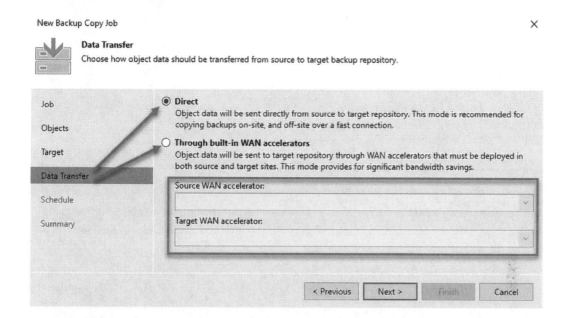

Figure 6.19 – The Data Transfer options to the backup target repository

6. Click **Next >** again to proceed to the **Schedule** section of the wizard, where you can set up a schedule for your job. Here, you can select **Any time (continuously)** or **During the following time periods only**. Once you have selected the option you require, click **Apply** to set up your job and move to the final **Summary** screen, as shown in the following screenshot:

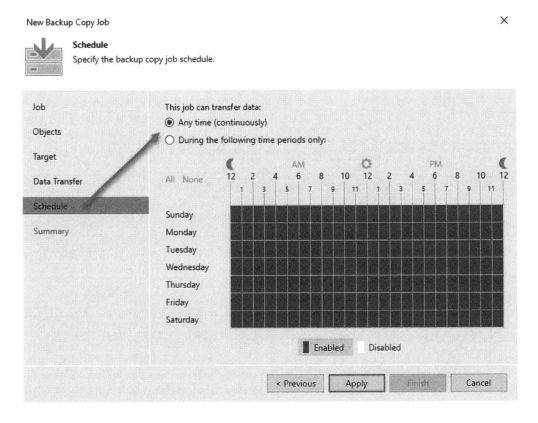

Figure 6.20 – The Schedule options for the backup copy job

7.   On the **Summary** screen, you can choose whether to enable the job by turning on the **Enable job when I click Finish** option and then clicking **Finish** to complete the job setup, as shown in the following screenshot. You can choose not to enable the job by removing the checkmark first if you prefer:

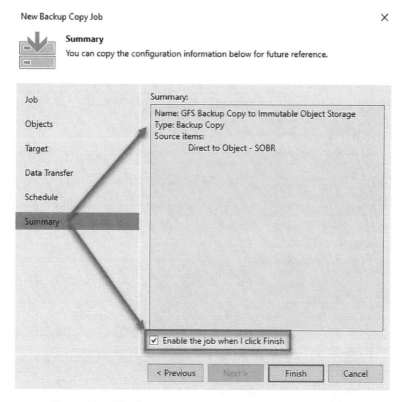

Figure 6.21 – The Summary screen and job enablement option

We have now set up a backup copy job that uses GFS to store additional weekly and monthly restore points directed to an immutable Wasabi repository. You will now have a second copy of your backup, which will also be in an immutable repository, a new feature for GFS backups.

As you can see, setting up GFS backup jobs for direct-to-object storage is pretty straightforward. We will now look at the last section of this chapter for the enhancements made to third-party integrations within the VBR v12 console.

Discovering third-party integrations within the console for Azure and Wasabi

Another significant VBR v12 console enhancement is how third-party integrations are carried out with object storage vendors. The two vendors that will be used as examples are Microsoft Azure and Wasabi when it comes to adding them for object storage, no matter the repository tier they will be used in – performance, capacity, or archive tiers.

You will see from the subsequent screenshots that Veeam gives you the selection options for these vendors, detailing logos and information relevant to that vendor:

Wasabi Object storage

When selecting to add Wasabi Object storage, you will see the following:

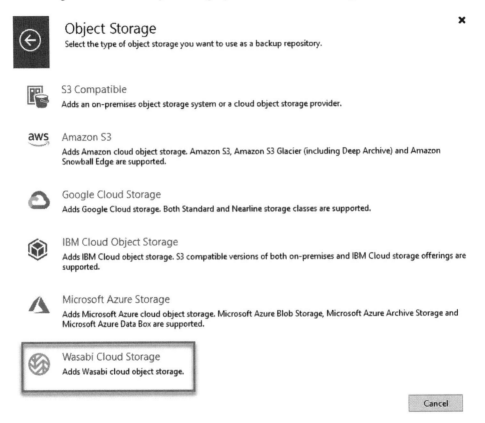

Figure 6.22 – The Wasabi Cloud Storage selection

Furthermore, the repository wizard has refined where you need to enter your **Region** and **Credentials** details – no more entering the Access Point URL as in the following screenshot:

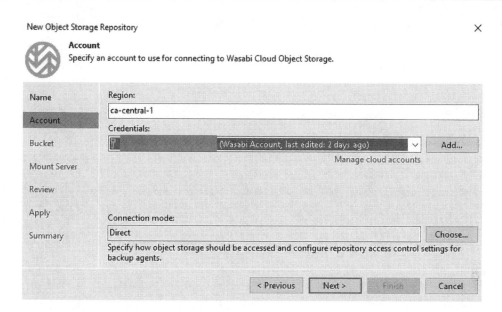

Figure 6.23 – Account requirements for adding Wasabi object storage

The following section shows Microsoft Azure storage.

Microsoft Azure Storage

When you add **Microsoft Azure Storage**, you will be presented with a further dialog to choose the type of storage, as shown in the following screenshot:

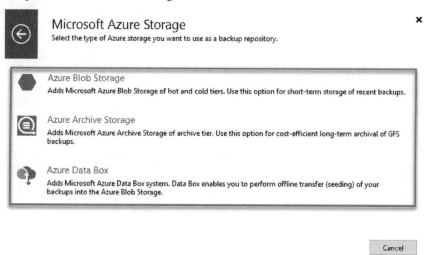

Figure 6.24 – The Microsoft Azure Storage types

Here, you have the **Azure Blob Storage**, **Azure Archive Storage**, and **Azure Data Box** storage options. This dialog tells you what types of object storage you can use with Microsoft Azure.

We have now looked at all topics within this chapter, so let's summarize what we have learned.

Summary

This chapter has reviewed direct-to-object storage and the newest enhancements. We looked at the new direct-to-object storage available within VBR v12. We reviewed configuring and setting up the new GFS backups to object storage with immutability. Finally, we looked at the enhancements to third-party integrations for Microsoft Azure and Wasabi object storage. After reading this chapter, you should have a much deeper understanding of the new direct-to-object storage options. You should also now understand how to configure GFS backups to immutable object storage within VBR v12. Lastly, you learned about the new third-party integrations for Microsoft Azure and Wasabi object storage.

Hopefully, you will now have a better understanding of the new object storage integrations and enhancements. The next chapter will look at what Veeam has done in v12 to enhance **network-attached storage** (**NAS**) backups.

Further reading

- Backup copy jobs – copy mode: `https://helpcenter.veeam.com/docs/backup/vsphere/backup_copy_name.html?ver=120`

- *Adding Wasabi Cloud Storage*: `https://helpcenter.veeam.com/docs/backup/vsphere/adding_wasabi_object_storage.html?ver=120`

- *Adding Azure Cloud Object storage*: `https://helpcenter.veeam.com/docs/backup/vsphere/adding_azure_object_storage.html?ver=120`

7

What's New in NAS Backup

This chapter will examine what's new in **Veeam Backup & Replication** (**VBR**) v12 with **network-attached storage** (**NAS**) backups. First, we will discuss how the archive copy mode and direct-to-object storage work with NAS backups. We will then discuss how now NAS backup can be sent to immutable repositories for backups. Next, we examine publishing a **network file system** (**NFS**) NAS backup as a **Server Message Block** (**SMB**) share for access. Finally, we will explore the health check options and the cloud helper appliance.

By the end of this chapter, you will understand what NAS backup enhancements are new in v12. You will also know their use cases and how they fit into your environment, whether you are using NAS backups now or in the future. Finally, you will better understand publishing an NFS backup as an SMB share, health check options, and the cloud helper appliance.

In this chapter, we will cover the following main topics:

- Understanding NAS backup – archive copy mode and direct-to-object storage
- Understanding NAS backup with immutability support
- Discovering NFS backup publishing as an SMB share
- Learning about health check features and the cloud helper appliance

Technical requirements

For this chapter, you should have VBR installed. If you followed along through the book, *Chapter 1, Installation – Best Practices and Optimizations*, covered the installation and optimization of VBR, which you can use in this chapter. Access to a NAS device will help reinforce many concepts covered in this chapter, but it is not required.

Understanding NAS backup – archive copy mode and direct-to-object storage

Within the VBR v12, you can add NAS shares to your inventory. Then you back them up to object storage and an archive repository for further retention. This process is accomplished when setting up your file copy job to include your NAS folders.

Based on the following screenshot, you can see where I have added my NFS share to the VBR v12 console to be able to back it up:

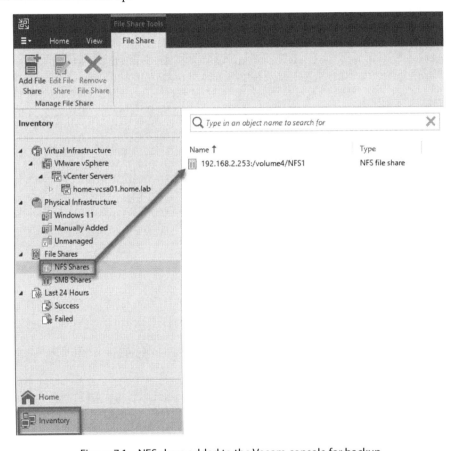

Figure 7.1 – NFS share added to the Veeam console for backup

While adding your NFS share on your NAS device, you have a wizard that walks you through setting things up. I will walk through the share I have already set up to show the screens for a NAS share:

1. The first screen of the **File Share** wizard is the **NFS File Share** screen, where you input the location of your NAS and share and set the **Advanced** options, as shown in the following screenshot:

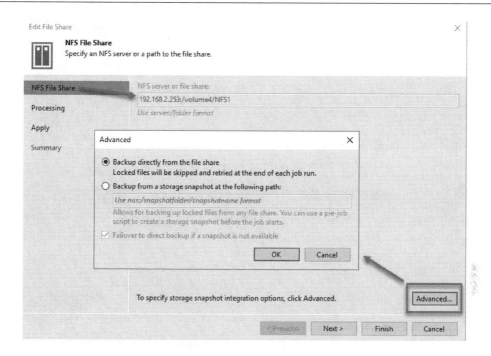

Figure 7.2 – The NFS File Share input and the Advanced options

2. After entering your information, click **Next >** to move to the **Processing** section to set up options, as in the following screenshot:

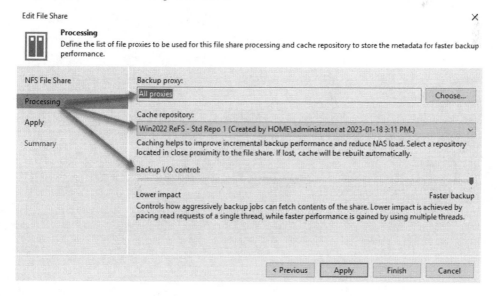

Figure 7.3 – The Processing options for file share

3. After setting the **Processing** options, click **Apply** to move to the **Apply** screen to make the changes (in my example) or add the file share. Click **Next >** to proceed to the **Summary** screen to review the settings, and then click **Finish** to complete the **File Share** wizard, as shown in the following screenshot:

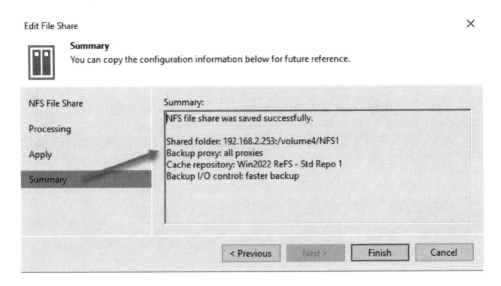

Figure 7.4 – The Summary screen for file share addition

We have now added the NFS share, which is the first step in the process of backing up your NAS device and shares. Let's now look at both direct-to-object storage and archive repository options.

With VBR v12, direct-to-object storage is a theme and movement that allows users to go directly to object storage without using block storage. Object storage allows for easier expansion for sizing over block storage. You can send to either on-premises object storage or offsite, another data center, or another object storage provider such as Wasabi.

Complete the following steps to set up a new file copy job, sending it directly to object storage and configuring an archival repository:

1. From the **Home** tab, you can right-click the job window and select **Backup | File share...** or use the **Backup Job** button in the toolbar:

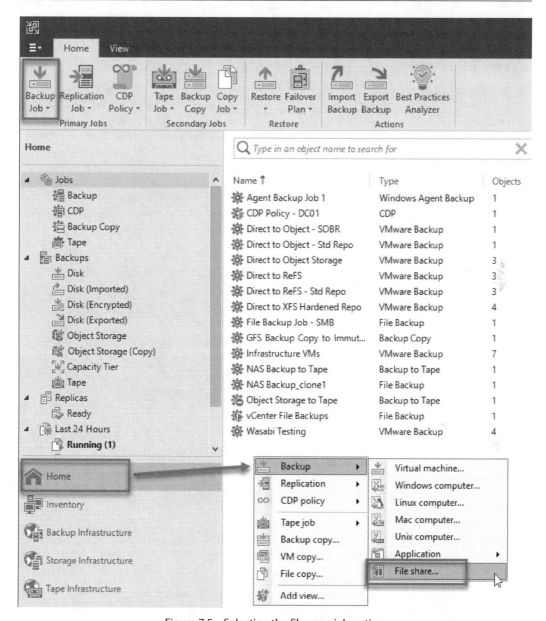

Figure 7.5 – Selecting the file copy job option

2. You are then presented with the **New File Backup Job** window. Enter the **Name** and **Description** values, then click **Next >** to proceed to the **Files and Folders** tab. You do have the option to mark this job as **High priority** as well if your backup window or SLA requires this, as in the following screenshot:

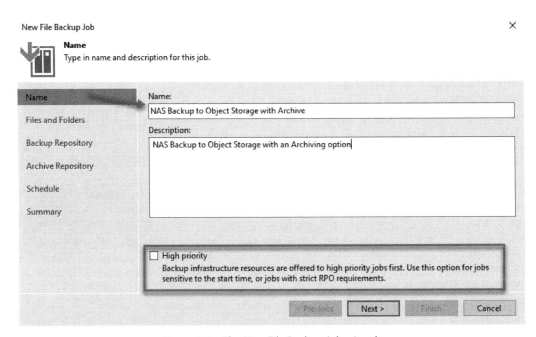

Figure 7.6 – The New File Backup Job wizard

3. You are now on the **File and Folders** screen in the wizard, where you can select your NFS share added in the preceding steps, as shown in the following screenshot:

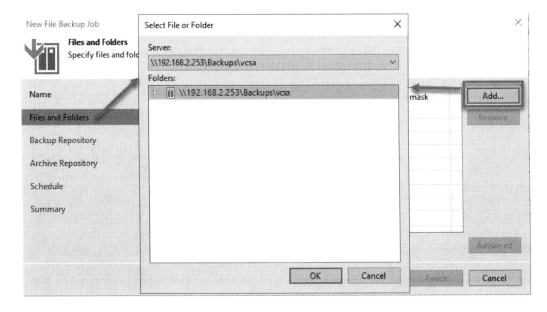

Figure 7.7 – The Select File or Folder window for the NFS share

4. After selecting your share and clicking **OK**, click **Next >** to move to the **Backup Repository** window, where you can choose an object storage repository for the direct-to-object option, as shown in *Figure 7.8*:

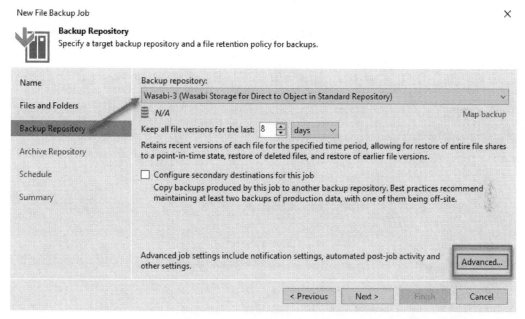

Figure 7.8 – Backup Repository selection for an object storage repository

> **Note**
> The default number of days to keep files is 28, which you can change to your desired configuration. You can also set advanced options such as file versions, **access control list** (**ACL**) handling, storage, and so on, from the **Advanced** button.

5.   After selecting your repository, click **Next >** to proceed to the **Archive Repository** tab, where you can set up an archival copy of your NAS backup, as shown in *Figure 7.9*:

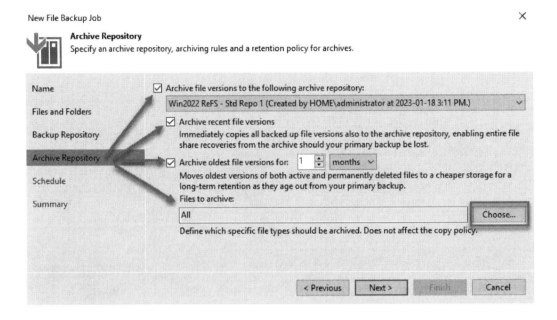

Figure 7.9 – Archive Repository and options selection

At this point in the wizard, you can set the following things:

- The archive repository location can be local, network, or internet-based block or object storage.

- You can turn on the **Archive recent file versions** option to make immediate copies of your backup data on the archive.

- You can turn on **Archive oldest file versions for:**, which allows you to set a retention period in months or years. This option will move the oldest backup in the chain to the archive repository and remove it from the primary storage to save space.

Lastly, the **Files to archive** option defaults to **All**, but you can click the **Choose…** button to select other options:

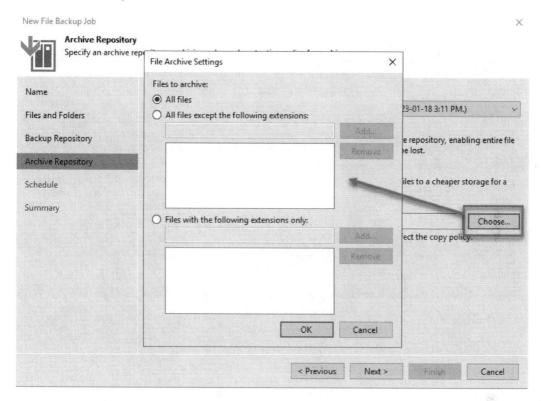

Figure 7.10 – Archive repository files to archive setting

6. After clicking **Next >**, you are then at the **Schedule** screen, where you can schedule your job to run. Click **Apply** to create your job, which presents the **Summary** screen, then click **Finish** to complete the wizard, as shown in *Figure 7.11*:

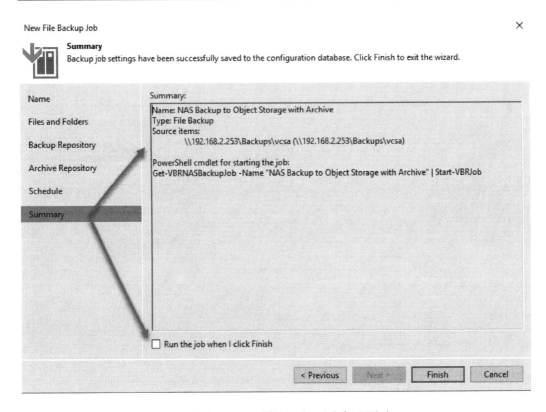

Figure 7.11 – Summary of file backup job for NAS share

> **Note**
> You can run your job immediately by turning on the **Run the job when I click Finish** checkbox, which will not wait for the scheduled time, instead running your job immediately.

We have covered both topics for this book section, which was direct-to-object storage and archive copy mode to a secondary repository. We will now examine how NAS backups can be sent to immutable storage for further protection.

Understanding NAS backup with immutability support

Something that goes along with the direct-to-object storage and archival support for NAS backups is another feature that is new in VBR v12, which is sending NAS backups to immutable repositories.

The process for this is similar to creating a NAS backup job as outlined in the preceding *Understanding NAS backup – archive copy mode and direct-to-object storage* section. The only difference is that when you come to the **Backup Repository** screen of the **New File Backup Job** wizard, you select an immutable repository to send your NAS backup data to, as shown in the following screenshot:

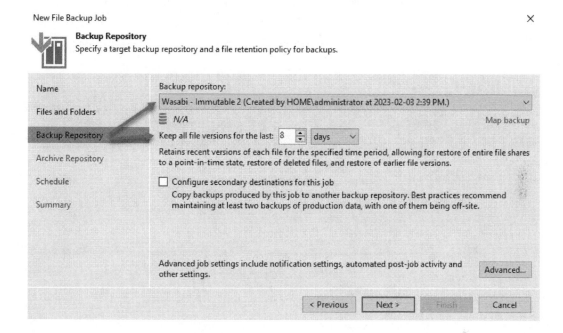

Figure 7.12 – Immutable repository selection for NAS backups

> **Note**
>
> For my example, I am using one of the Wasabi repositories I have added to my console that has immutability turned on.

After your backup completes, you will notice on the summary screen a line that indicates that immutability has been set, as shown in the following screenshot:

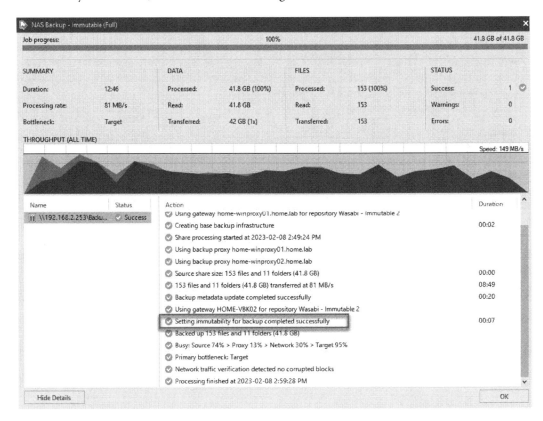

Figure 7.13 – Immutability has been set for NAS backups on the repository

So you are now protected with the number of versions of the file retention you select and the added benefit of immutability. To test the immutable feature, if we try to delete the backups from within the Veeam console, we will see in the status window that VBR v12 cannot delete the files due to them being immutable. The following screenshot shows that the deletion of the NAS backups is not allowed due to the immutability setting:

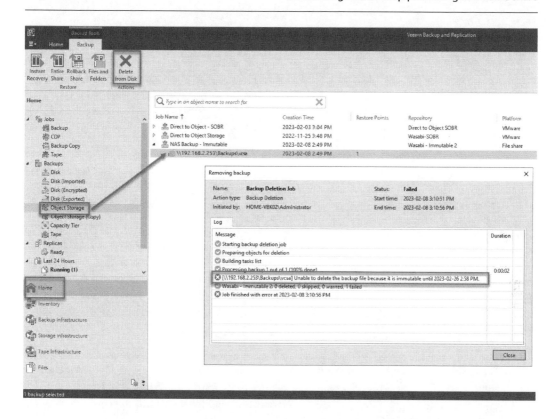

Figure 7.14 – Deletion of NAS backup not allowed due to immutability

So from the examples given here, we can see that sending NAS backups to immutable storage gives you an added layer of security and protection for your backups.

Now that we have covered immutable NAS backups, let's look at how we can publish an NFS backup as an SMB share to allow user access without having to restore.

Discovering NFS backup publishing as an SMB share

When you want to allow users access to a NAS backup, a new feature within VBR v12 will mount the recovery point selected and then access it over SMB as a file share. You also control the permissions when the backup is published, including the owner and user permissions.

You must select the **Instant Recovery** option for your NAS backup stored on disk to accomplish this task. Follow these steps for an example of this:

1. Within the console, under the **Home** tab, please select the location of your backups and highlight it. Click the **Instant Recovery** button in the toolbar to start the **Instant File Share Recovery** wizard, as shown in *Figure 7.15*:

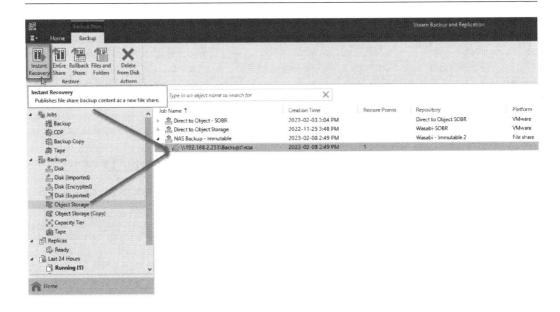

Figure 7.15 – Instant Recovery selection for backup

2.   The **Instant File Share Recovery** wizard will start and show you the selected NAS backup you will recover. You can also select another restore point using the **Point...** button if you have more than one, which I do not. Click **Next >** to proceed to the **Mount Servers** screen when ready, as shown in the following screenshot:

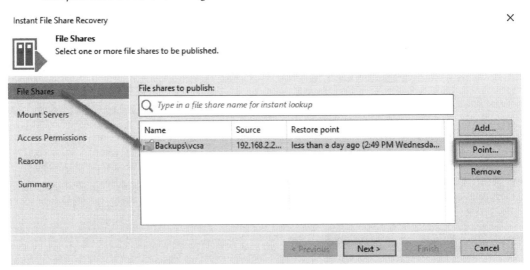

Figure 7.16 – File share selection for recovery

3. On the **Mount Servers** screen, you can allow VBR v12 to automatically select the server to use or manually select a mount server. For this example, we will use **Automatic selection**. Click **Next >** to proceed, as shown in the following screenshot:

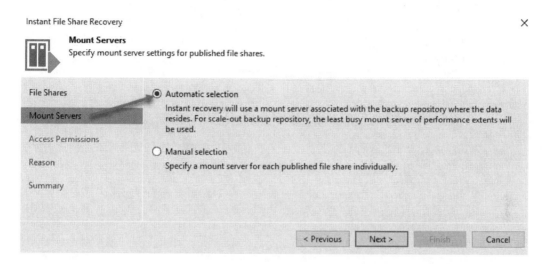

Figure 7.17 – Mount server selection – automatic or manual

4. On the **Access Permissions** tab, you can set the security for the new SMB share created on the mount server. You can select the **Set Owner...** and **Permissions...** options. You can also see the SMB share path that will be created under the **File share** column, as shown in the following screenshot:

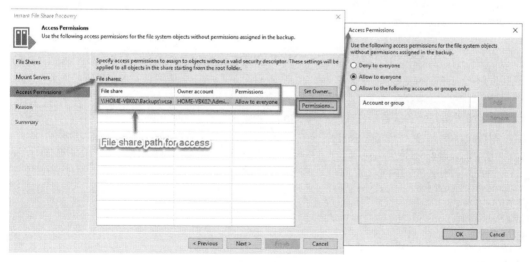

Figure 7.18 – Access Permissions and file share path

5.   After clicking **Next** >, you are at the **Reason** page where you can enter a descriptive reason for the restore or select to not show this dialog again with the checkbox at the bottom. Click **Next** > to proceed to the **Summary** screen. Note that you will see the following popup when the **Permissions…** option is set to **Allow to everyone**, as shown in the following screenshot:

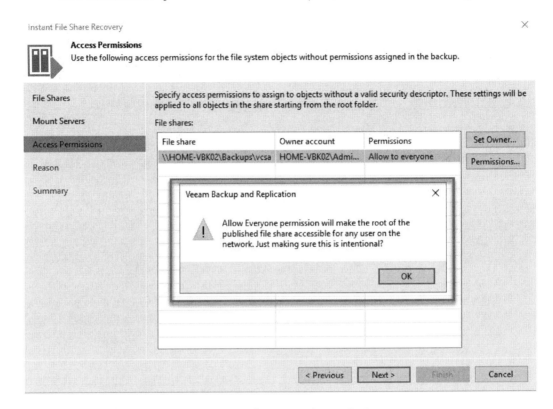

Figure 7.19 – Warning before proceeding to the Reason page

> **Note**
>
> Be sure if you want to grant everyone permission that this is your intention, as anyone on the network can access the share once published. It is better to use the **Permissions…** button to set specific user permissions. For this example, I am using the **Allow to everyone** option.

The next screen is the **Reason** page, where you describe why you are running the recovery job:

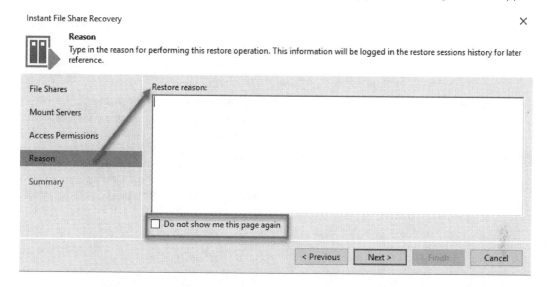

Figure 7.20 – The Reason page for the restore and the option to disable it

6. Once you've entered a reason, click **Next >** to view the **Summary** screen. Then click **Finish** to start publishing the restore point as an SMB share, as shown in the following screenshot:

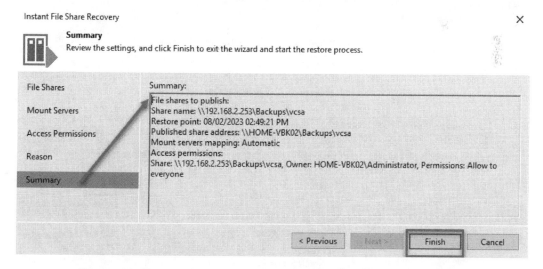

Figure 7.21 – The Summary screen and the Finish button to complete the wizard

> **Note**
>
> In the **Summary** screen, you can again see the SMB share path on the **Published share address:** line, which is how to access it.

After the wizard completes, you can see the restore point mounted within the VBR v12 console on the **Home** tab, as shown in the following screenshot:

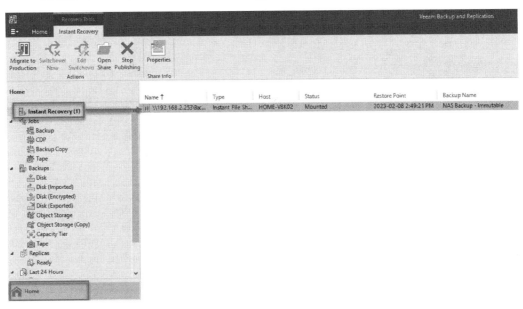

Figure 7.22 – The Instant Recovery restore published for access

7. To access the published SMB share, navigate to the \\HOME-VBK02\Backups\vcsa location from another server within your network or even on the local VBR v12 server:

Figure 7.23 – Accessing the SMB share over the network

8. To now complete the restore process, you will need to use the **Stop Publishing** button in the VBR v12 console, which allows you to do the following:

    - Stop the sharing

    - Unmount the backup from the mount server

    - Stop the instant recovery session

9. When you click the **Stop Publishing** button, you will see a popup asking whether you want to stop publishing the share, click **Yes**, as shown in the following screenshot:

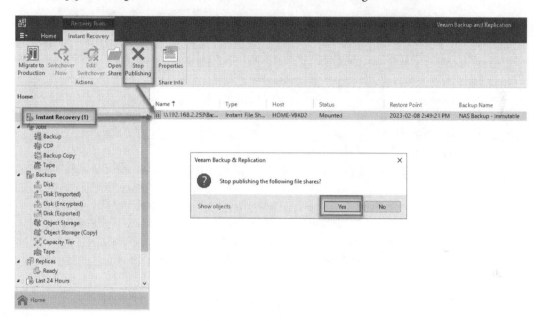

Figure 7.24 – Stop Publishing and the confirmation dialog

After the mounted restore point is unpublished, you see a status and confirmation window. You will notice that the **Instant Recovery** section in *Figure 7.24* has now been removed from the console window, as shown in *Figure 7.25*:

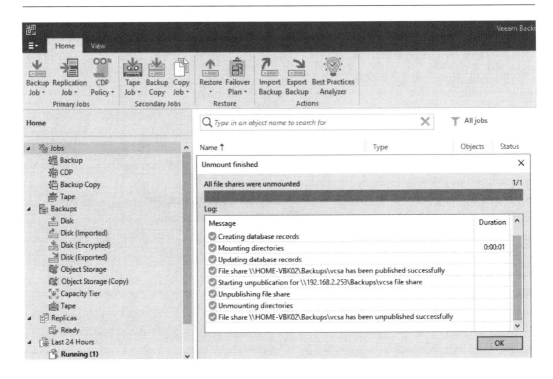

Figure 7.25 – Instant file recovery unpublished

Now that we have looked at the SMB share option for NAS backups, let's explore our final topic of this chapter regarding the health check features and the cloud helper appliance.

Learning about health check features and the cloud helper appliance

For this last section of the book, I will be discussing the following two features within the VBR v12 environment:

- The health check utility
- The cloud helper appliance

The health check utility was also present in VBR v11; however, I wanted to give some details regarding checking your NAS backup files covered in the preceding sections of this chapter.

The health check utility

The health check utility checks the restore point consistency and the ability to restore from your backups. In addition, it will perform a **cyclic redundancy check (CRC)** on the metadata and a hash check on the data blocks to validate their integrity.

To run a health check on your NAS backup, do the following:

1. From within the VBR v12 console, go to the **Home** tab and then the **Jobs** screen. Right-click on your NAS backup job, select **Run health check**, or use the **Run Health Check** button in the toolbar, as shown in the following screenshot:

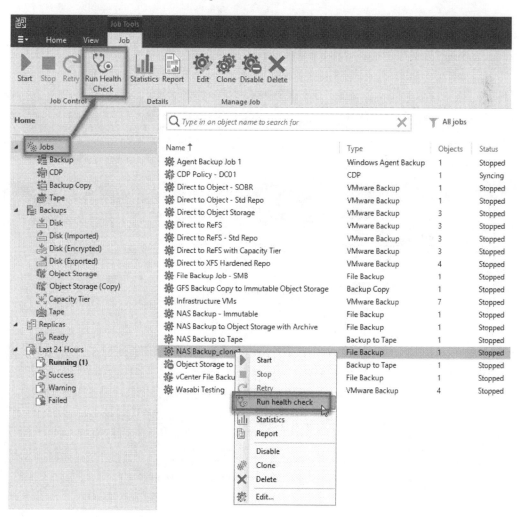

Figure 7.26 – The Run health check options

2. After you select to run the health check, a status window will appear on the screen showing you the progress of the health check, as shown in the following screenshot:

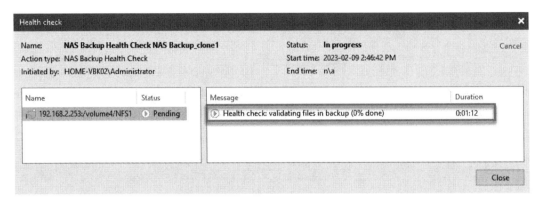

Figure 7.27 – The Health check status dialog

3. Once the health check is complete, the **Health check** dialog window will show a **Success** status. You can review the health check status and click **Close** to close the dialog, as shown in the following screenshot:

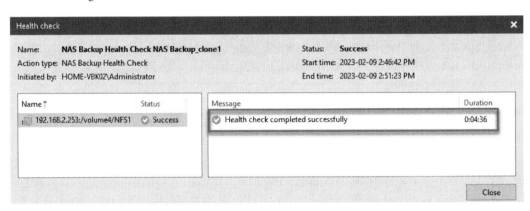

Figure 7.28 – Successful health check status

> **Note**
> Had problems been detected, the status window would have shown more details for you regarding the issues, and you could have run the **Repair backup** option.

The following depiction of the **Repair backup** option is directly from the link in the *Further reading* section at the end of this chapter. It shows inconsistencies in the NAS backup and the backup repair option:

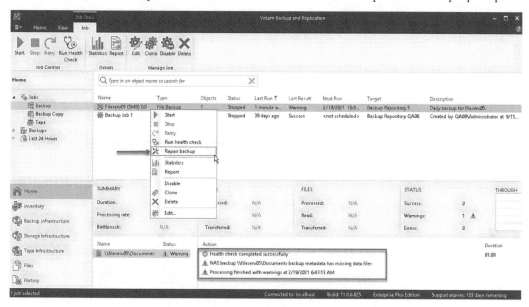

Figure 7.29 – Issues detected and the Repair backup option

As you can see, the health check is an excellent tool for checking your NAS backups to ensure consistency and the ability to restore them without issues. You can even repair backups, as shown in the preceding example. Now let us look at another component in VBR v12, which is the cloud helper appliance.

> **NAS to tape**
> VBR v12 also allows NAS backups to be sent directly to tape. Should this be used in addition to backups on disk, be sure to configure the jobs carefully. If a backup job is created with a NAS share directly to disk and a NAS share directly to tape, then there will be two licenses consumed for both jobs. Instead, use the previously-explained archive repository for multiple copies or a NAS job that is sent to tape with the source being the backup of the NAS share to disk.

The cloud helper appliance

What is a cloud helper appliance, you might be asking yourself? It is a small Linux virtual machine that is used during the restore of Linux servers to any of the following cloud vendors:

- Microsoft Azure
- Amazon AWS
- Google Cloud

For each of the mentioned vendors, when set up within the VBR v12 environment, a small Linux appliance is deployed to restore Linux-based virtual machines to the cloud provider. If you have multiple locations for your cloud provider, then you will need to ensure that a cloud helper appliance is installed in each location to ensure that you can restore.

Let's use Microsoft Azure to deploy the cloud helper appliance for this example. The following is how to complete the task:

1. From within the VBR v12 console, click the hamburger menu, select **Credentials and Passwords**, then select **Cloud Credentials**, as shown in the following screenshot:

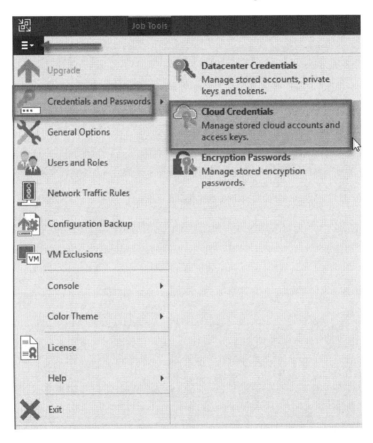

Figure 7.30 – Adding Cloud Credentials for the helper appliance

2. In the **Manage Cloud Credentials** dialog, select the **Add...** button and choose **Microsoft Azure compute account...** as shown in the following screenshot:

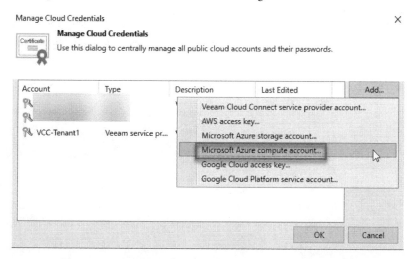

Figure 7.31 – Selecting Microsoft Azure compute account...

3. The **Microsoft Azure Compute Account** wizard starts. Enter a name and description for your account and click **Next**, as shown in *Figure 7.32*:

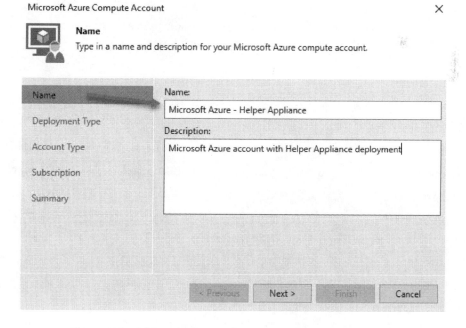

Figure 7.32 – Adding the Microsoft Azure Compute Account wizard

4. The next screen is the **Deployment Type** screen, where you choose between **Microsoft Azure** and **Microsoft Azure Stack**. Make your selection and click **Next** to proceed:

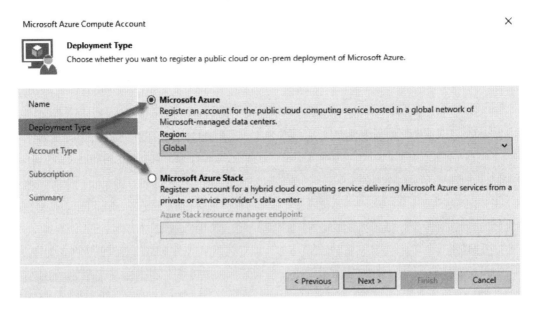

Figure 7.33 – Deployment type selection

5. The **Account Type** screen allows you to choose between **Create a new account** or **Use the existing account**. Make your selection and then click **Next** to proceed:

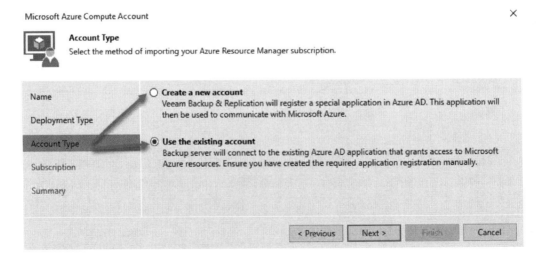

Figure 7.34 – Account Type selection

6. When you select **Create a new account**, the **Subscription** screen allows you to enter a code for the wizard to set things up for you. You also turn on the **Linux support** option for the cloud helper appliance deployment and click **Next** to proceed, as shown in the following screenshot:

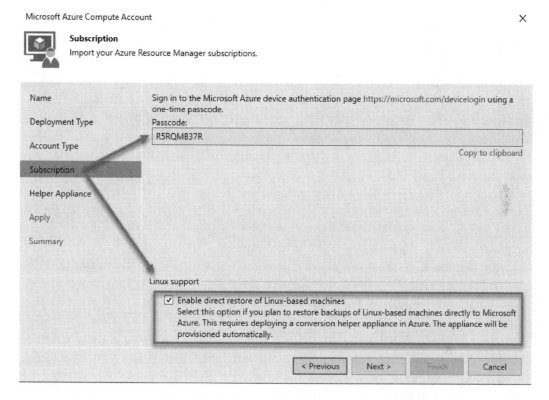

Figure 7.35 – The Subscription account creation and Linux support enablement

7. The **Helper Appliance** screen is where you add your appliance settings. Once done, click **OK**, and then click **Apply** when ready to apply the settings to your Microsoft Azure account:

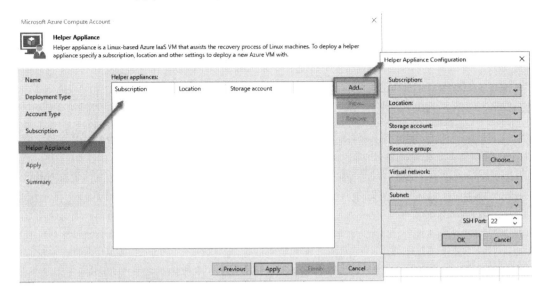

Figure 7.36 – The Helper Appliance configuration screen

> **Note**
> Due to not having a valid subscription, I cannot complete the wizard, but if you do have a subscription, then after clicking **Apply**, you are directed to the **Summary** screen containing the details. Click **Finish** to exit the wizard.

After you complete the wizard, you will see your new **Microsoft Azure compute** account listed in the **Manage Cloud Credentials** window:

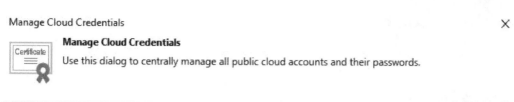

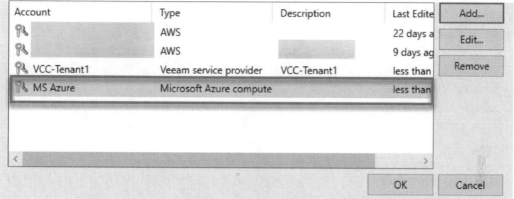

Figure 7.37 – Manage Cloud Credentials showing Microsoft Azure compute

We have now covered the section on health checks and using the cloud helper appliance for Microsoft Azure. Let's now summarize this chapter.

Summary

This chapter reviewed new enhancements for NAS backups. First, we looked at the archive copy mode for NAS backups and the direct-to-object storage option. We also reviewed the ability to use immutable repositories for NAS backups. We then looked at how to publish a NAS backup as an SMB share for user access. Lastly, we discussed the ability to run a health check on a NAS backup and how a cloud helper appliance is used with the current cloud providers.

After reading this chapter, you should have a much deeper understanding of the NAS backup enhancements and what's new in v12.

Hopefully, you now have a better idea of NAS backups. The next and final chapter will examine **continuous data protection** (**CDP**) and Veeam Cloud Connect and how they can be leveraged together.

Further reading

- *Health Check*: `https://helpcenter.veeam.com/docs/backup/vsphere/health_check_nas_backup.html?ver=120`

- *Helper Appliance – Microsoft Azure*: `https://helpcenter.veeam.com/docs/backup/vsphere/restore_azure_linux.html?ver=120`

- *Helper Appliance – Amazon AWS*: `https://helpcenter.veeam.com/docs/backup/vsphere/restore_amazon_proxy_appliance.html?ver=120`

- *Helper Appliance – Google Cloud*: `https://helpcenter.veeam.com/docs/backup/vsphere/restore_google_proxy_appliances.html?ver=120`

CDP and Veeam Cloud Connect

Veeam Backup & Replication v12 has a great feature called **Continuous Data Protection** (CDP), which will be the focus of this chapter, along with touching on **Veeam Cloud Connect** (VCC). We will investigate how to use CDP on **VMware Cloud Director** (**vCD**) within VCC. Next, you will learn how to leverage CDP to set disaster recovery from vCD to vCD. Finally, we will look at Veeam Cloud Connect, including the new Instant VM Recovery feature.

By the end of this chapter, you will have discovered how CDP works with vCD in a VCC environment. You will also be able to explain how you can use CDP to send data from one vCD to another vCD. You will also know more about VCC, including the Instant VM Recovery feature.

In this chapter, we're going to cover the following main topics:

- Discovering CDP to vCD in Veeam Cloud Connect
- Exploring CDP with vCD to vCD
- Investigating Instant VM Recovery within Veeam Cloud Connect

Technical requirements

For this chapter, you should have Veeam Backup & Replication installed. If you have followed along through the book, *Chapter 1, Installation – Best Practices and Optimizations*, covered the installation and optimization of Veeam Backup & Replication, which you can leverage in sections of this chapter.

Discovering CDP to vCD in Veeam Cloud Connect

Continuous Data Protection (CDP) is a way for you to protect your virtual machines with a to-the-second **Recovery Time Objective** (**RTO**) based on your required **Service-Level Agreement** (**SLA**). It will also provide the minimum RTO for your mission-critical servers because the replica VMs created in the process can be powered up at any time.

Four components make up the CDP infrastructure, and they are the following:

- **Backup Server** – The backup server is the CDP coordinator that ensures things are communicating and working between the CDP proxy servers and the VMware hosts

- **CDP Proxy** – The CDP proxy replicates the VMs from the source host to the destination host

- **Source and Target Hosts** – There is a source host of the VM you want to protect with CDP and the target host, which is where the replica VM will be created

- **I/O Filters** – Each host in both the source and target cluster requires an I/O filter driver to be installed, which works in conjunction with the CDP proxy servers for the replication

The CDP infrastructure looks like this:

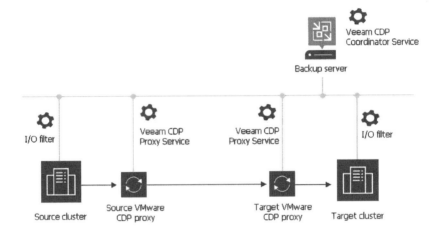

Figure 8.1 – CDP infrastructure components

> **Note**
>
> For further information on CDP, please see the *Further reading* section and check *Chapter 3* of *Mastering Veeam Backup & Replication: Second Edition*.

When sending to Veeam Cloud Connect, there are two ways in which you can use CDP:

- **Veeam Cloud Connect without VMware Cloud Director** – This method uses VMware vCenter and hardware plans created within the console, which are assigned to the tenants for Replication resources

- **Veeam Cloud Connect with VMware Cloud Director** – This method installs the I/O filter drivers into the tenant vCD to use CDP for replication to the Cloud Director tenant

Now let's leverage CDP with Veeam Cloud Connect using the VMware Cloud Director method. You first need to contact a **Veeam Certified Service Provider** (**VCSP**) to be set up with Veeam Cloud Connect. You can find a partner using the following site: `https://vee.am/splookup`

> **Note**
> You can search for services offered by type, country, and Veeam competency levels.

Once you have signed up for Veeam Cloud Connect services with a provider, they must create a vCloud Director tenant within the Veeam Cloud Connect console. This step is completed after setting up a tenant within the VMware Cloud Director environment first.

The tenant setup will look similar to this on the service provider side:

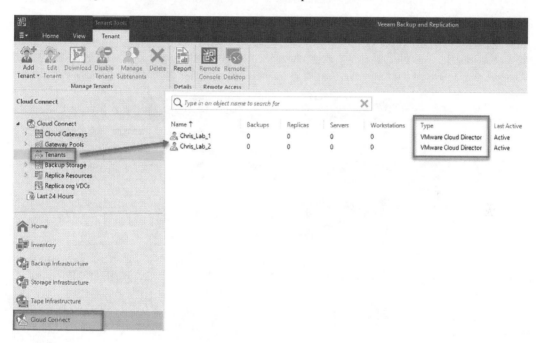

Figure 8.2 – VMware Cloud Director tenant setup

After the tenant is created, you will then have **Replica org VDCs** resources on the Veeam Cloud Connect side:

Figure 8.3 – Replica org VDCs for each tenant

We have covered the prerequisites for getting started with CDP for VMware Cloud Director. Let us now look at how you configure your Veeam Backup & Replication v12 server to set up CDP policies to VMware Cloud Director at the service provider.

To set up CDP to go from your on-premises Veeam Backup & Replication v12 server to the Veeam Cloud Connect provider, you must ensure that you have configured a CDP proxy within your environment. This process is carried out on the **Backup Infrastructure** tab under the **Backup Proxies** section:

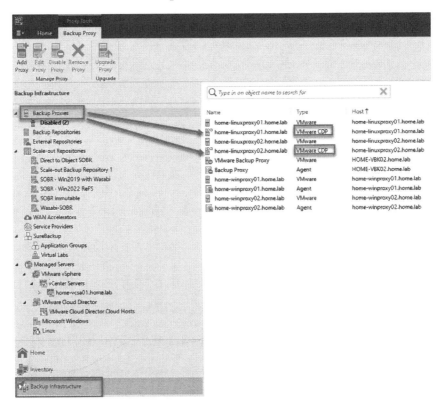

Figure 8.4 – CDP proxy setup in the Backup Proxies section

After you have created your CDP proxy servers, you can then create a CDP Policy job within the **Home** tab under **Jobs** using these steps:

1. Right-click in the job window on the right side of the console or use the **CDP Policy** button in the toolbar to start the **VMware vSphere** policy wizard.

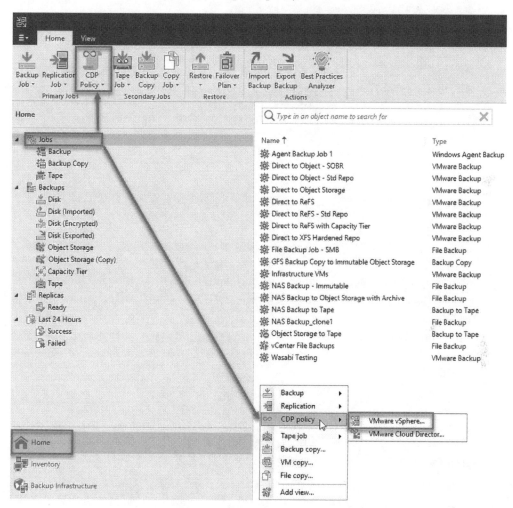

Figure 8.5 – CDP policy wizard for VMware vSphere

2. You then will have the **New CDP Policy** wizard start, where you can enter your name and description, and select advanced options.

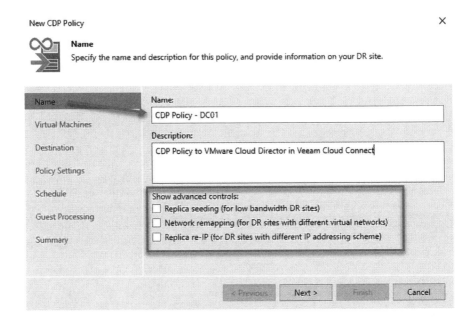

Figure 8.6 – New CDP Policy wizard

3. Enter your job's name and a description to ensure you know what servers are getting replicated, and select the advanced options required. Click **Next** when completed to move to the **Virtual Machines** section.

4. You will use the **Add…** button to select the virtual machines you want to be replicated. Once the servers are selected, click the **Add** button to place them in the job and click **Next** to move to the **Destination** section.

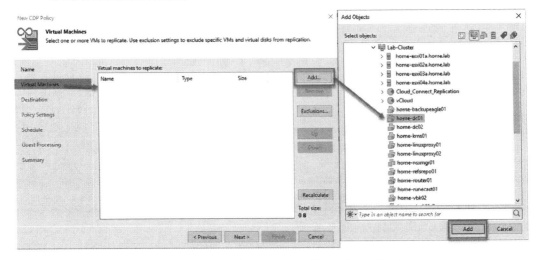

Figure 8.7 – Selecting the virtual machine(s) for replication

The following figure shows the screen after clicking the **Add** button to revert to the wizard:

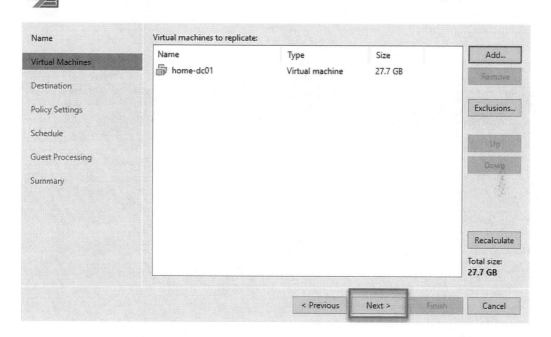

Figure 8.8 – Virtual machine(s) selected for CDP replication

5. Within the **Destination** section, you will select the Veeam Cloud Connect tenant to replicate to VMware Cloud Director. Click the **Add** button and select **Cloud host…**.

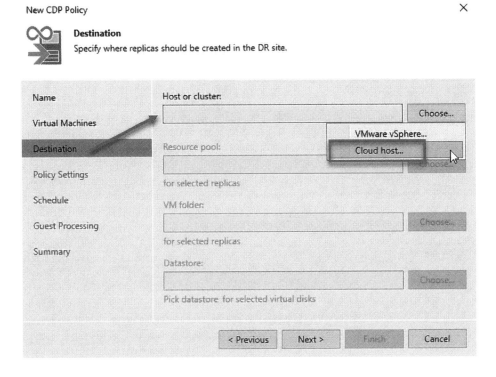

Figure 8.9 – Destination section where you select Cloud host

6. After clicking **Cloud host…**, you will choose the tenant created on Veeam Cloud Connect on the provider side, which was added to the Veeam Backup & Replication v12 console.

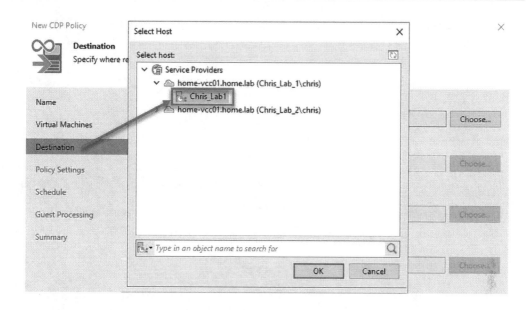

Figure 8.10 – Selecting the tenant from the service provider

7. After choosing the tenant from the **Service Providers** list, the **Destination** section of the wizard will get populated. Click **Next** to proceed to the **Policy Settings** section of the wizard.

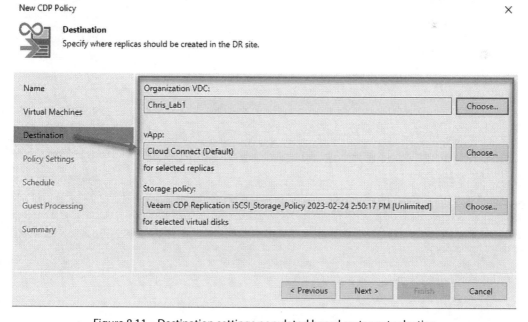

Figure 8.11 – Destination settings populated based on tenant selection

8. You will select your **Source proxy**, **Replica mapping**, and **Advanced** options in the **Policy Settings** section. Once all settings have been chosen, click **Next** to proceed to the **Schedule** section.

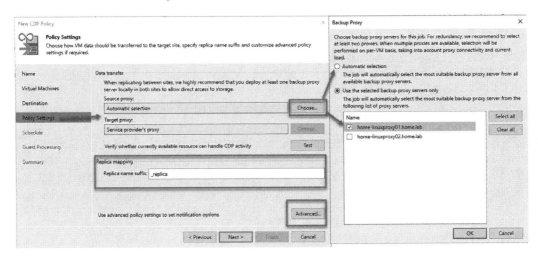

Figure 8.12 – Policy Settings selections

Note

You cannot change the **Target proxy** option since this will be a CDP proxy on the service provider side configured in the Veeam Cloud Connect console.

---

9. In the **Schedule** section, you will select your **Recovery Point Objective (RPO)**, **Short-term retention**, and **Long-term retention** settings. Click **Next** once these settings are complete to move to the **Guest Processing** section.

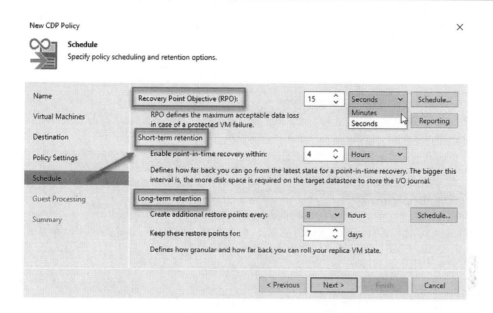

Figure 8.13 – Schedule settings for CDP policy

> **Note**
>
> The RPO setting can get set to minutes or seconds, and the short-term retention can be hours or minutes. Remember that if you use seconds, the system will be busy with activity, and the RPO may not be met. It would be best to determine what you want as your RPO/RTO to set these correctly for your organization.

10. You can select **Enable application-aware processing** on the **Guest Processing** tab to enable application-consistent backups, such as a domain controller. If you do not turn on this option, the VM will be crash-consistent instead. Once the options are set, click **Next** to move to the **Summary** section.

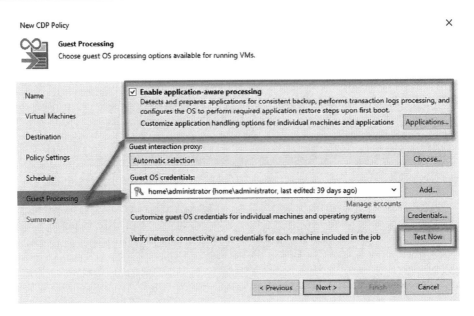

Figure 8.14 – Guest Processing options

11. In the **Summary** section, you can review all settings for your **New CDP Policy** wizard and select **Enable policy when I click Finish**, which will turn on the **CDP Policy** job. Click **Finish** if all settings meet your expectations or use the **Previous** button to go back to make adjustments.

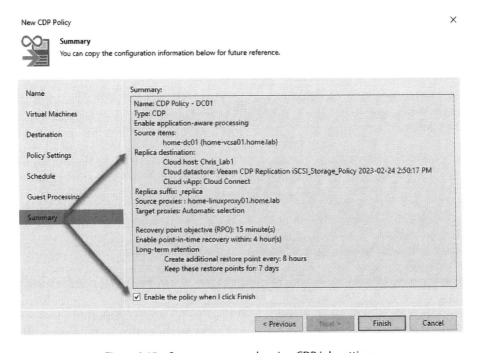

Figure 8.15 – Summary screen showing CDP job settings

12. After clicking **Finish**, the **CDP Policy** job will be created, and you can monitor it within the console.

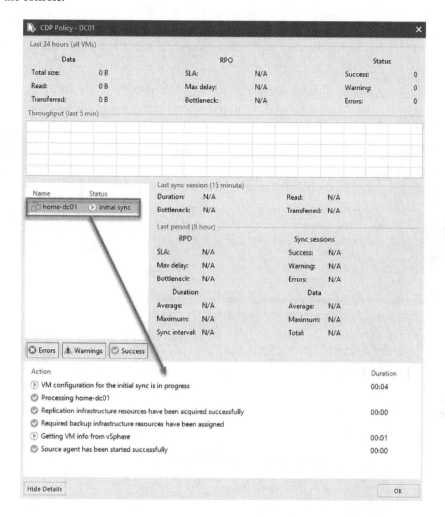

Figure 8.16 – CDP Policy monitoring from within the console

You should now understand the CDP requirements for sending replicas to VMware Cloud Director, including the CDP proxy servers, which communicate between your on-premises infrastructure and the Veeam Cloud Connect infrastructure on the service provider side. We will now look at how the CDP process works from one VMware Cloud Director to another, not using Veeam Cloud Connect.

Exploring CDP with vCD to vCD

As previously discussed, you can create CDP policy jobs to send your workloads to Veeam Cloud Connect on the Service Provider side, but what if you want to have CDP work with VMware Cloud Director between two sites or data centers? This process allows you to set up CDP to use vCD to vCD instead.

The following steps will walk through configuring a CDP job that will send data from one vApp in the VMware Cloud Director tenant to another vApp in another VMware Cloud Director tenant, whether in the same location/data center or a different location/data center:

1. The first step is to ensure you have added the VMware Cloud Director servers to the Veeam Backup & Replication v12 console. This process is accomplished from the **Backup Infrastructure** tab and by clicking the **Add Server** button, then **VMware vSphere**, and then **Cloud Director**.

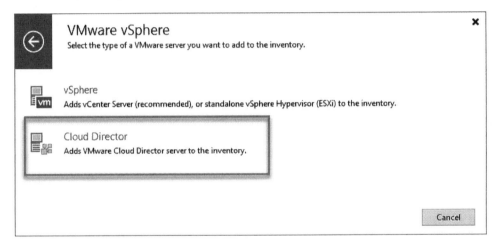

Figure 8.17 – Cloud Director option

2. Once you follow the wizard and complete it, you will see your VMware Cloud Director servers added to the console.

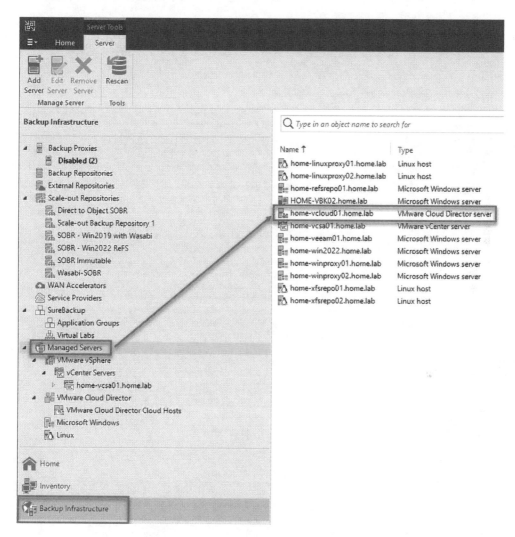

Figure 8.18 – VMware Cloud Director server added

3. Now, click on the **Home** tab, and under the **Jobs** section of the tree, right-click and click **CDP Policy** > **VMware Cloud Director…**, or use the **CDP Policy** button in the toolbar.

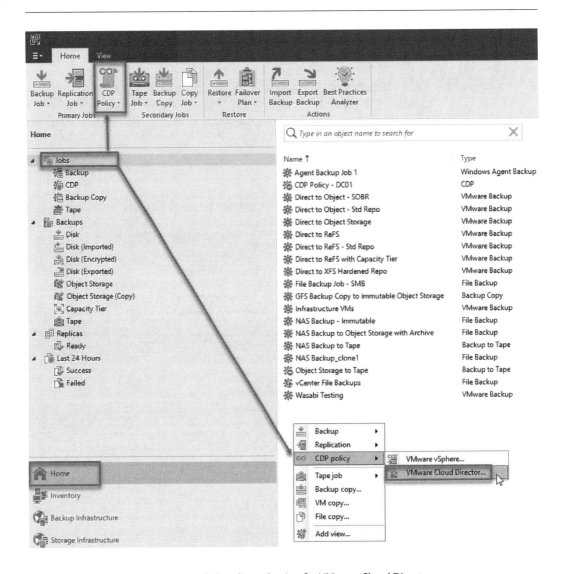

Figure 8.19 – CDP policy selection for VMware Cloud Director

4.   The **New VMware Cloud Director CDP Policy** wizard will launch. The first step is to type in a name and description and select any required advanced features based on your setup. Click **Next** to move to the **vApps** screen.

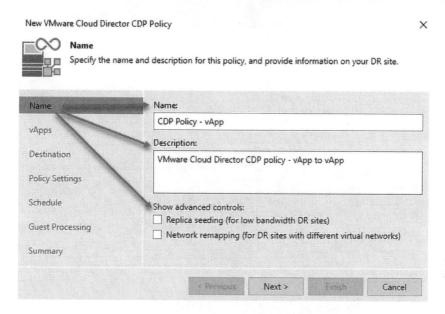

Figure 8.20 – Initial settings for VMware Cloud Director CDP Policy

5.   On the **vApps** screen, click the **Add…** button to choose the vApp you will replicate using CDP to the **Destination**. Click the **OK** button to add the vApp, then click **Next** to go to the **Destination** screen.

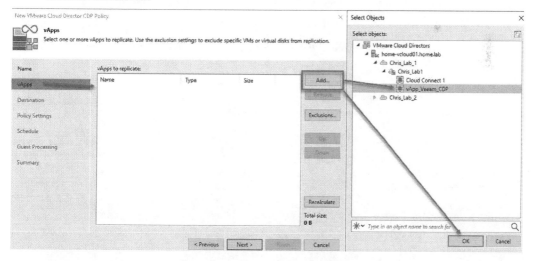

Figure 8.21 – vApp selection screen

6.   Select the VMware Cloud Director tenant on the **Destination** screen to replicate your servers using CDP. Click the **Choose…** button, select the tenant, and then click the **OK** button. The

Storage policy option chosen is the default one within VMware Cloud Director for the tenant, but you can use the **Choose…** button to change this. Once both options are selected, click **Next** to move to the **Policy Settings** tab.

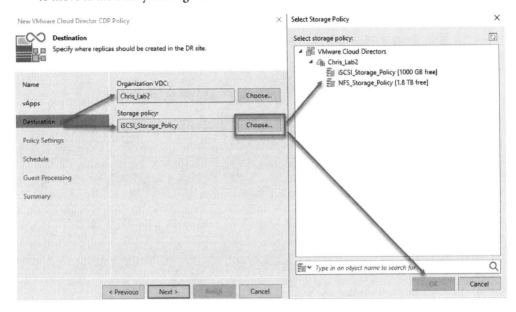

Figure 8.22 – Changing the Storage policy if required

7. The **Policy Settings** screen is where you select your **Source proxy**, **Target proxy**, and **Replica mapping** settings, and select your notification settings with the **Advanced…** button. Make the necessary changes and click **Next** to move to the **Schedule** screen.

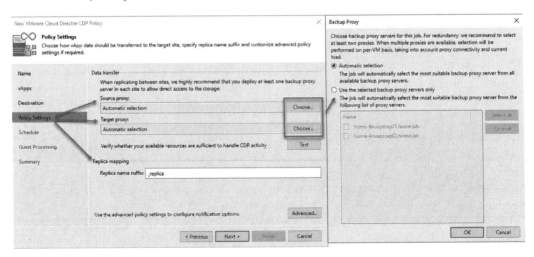

Figure 8.23 – Policy Settings screen

> **Note**
>
> You can use the **Test** button to check your configuration for the proxy servers to show whether you have the requirements for CDP activity.

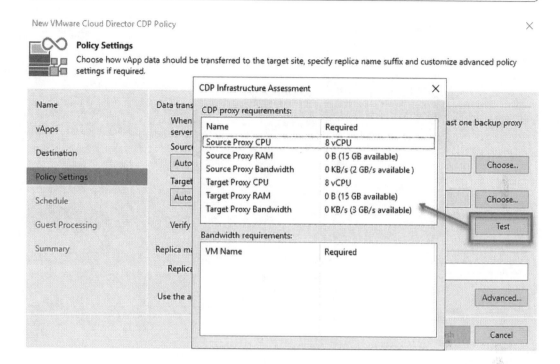

Figure 8.24 – Testing for CDP resources

8. On the **Schedule** screen, you set up **Recovery point objective (RPO)**, **Short-term retention**, and **Long-term retention**. The RPO can get set to **Minutes** or **Seconds** and **Short-term retention** to **Hours** or **Minutes**. Select your options, then click **Next** to move to the **Guest Processing** tab.

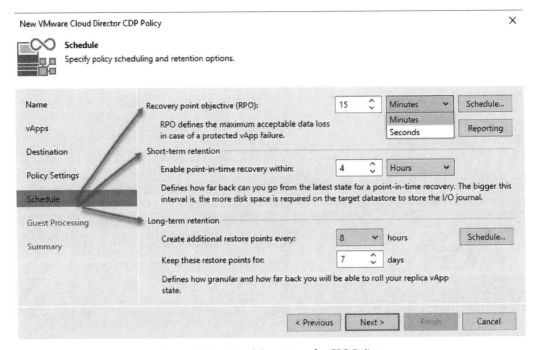

Figure 8.25 – Schedule settings for CDP Policy

> **Note**
>
> The RPO setting can get set to minutes or seconds, and the short-term retention can be hours
> or minutes. Remember that if you use seconds, the system will be busy with activity, and the
> RPO may not be achieved. It would be best to determine what you want as your RPO/RTO to
> set these correctly for your organization.

9. On the **Guest Processing** tab, you can turn on application-aware processing. Select the options
    required and click **Next** to move to the **Summary** screen.

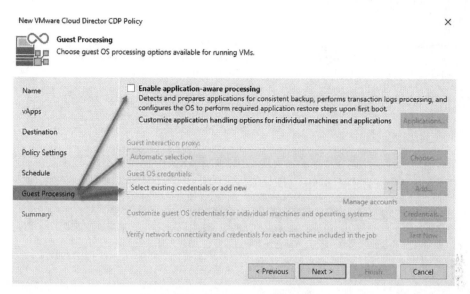

Figure 8.26 – Guest Processing options

10. The **Summary** page will show the settings for your CDP policy, and you can select the **Run the job when I click Finish** option. Click the **Finish** button to complete the setup and create the job, which can then be monitored in the console.

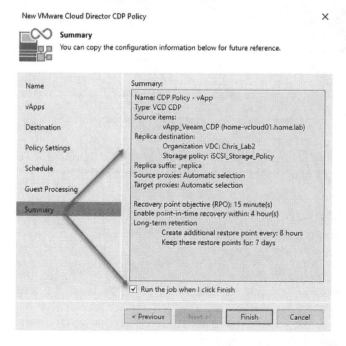

Figure 8.27 – Summary screen and the option to run the job when finished

As the job runs, you can monitor it from the console, as shown:

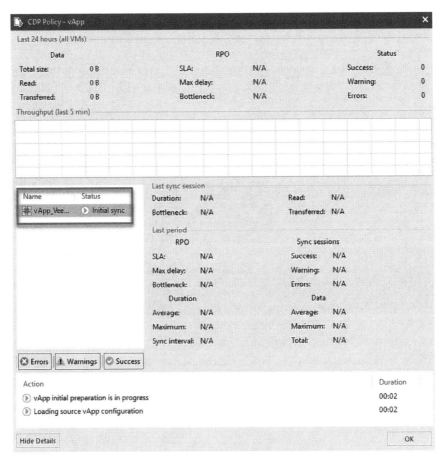

Figure 8.28 – Monitoring CDP Policy for VMware Cloud Director

Now that we have looked at using CDP for vCD to vCD, the last topic we will cover is the ability for instant VM recovery within the Veeam Cloud Connect console.

Investigating Instant VM Recovery within Veeam Cloud Connect

Another enhancement in Veeam Backup & Replication v12 that will help Service Providers out is conducting instant VM recovery from within the console for any tenants sending backups to the Cloud Connect repository. Prior to Veeam Backup & Replication v12, this was not possible for Service Providers, but with the feature introduced in v12, it is possible for a Service Provider to recover any VM for a client within their environment.

I will use a sample tenant I set up within the Veeam Cloud Connect console: VCC_Tenant. A backup job was created to send a virtual machine backup to the VCC server to conduct the instant VM recovery process. The process is as follows, and is done from the Veeam Cloud Connect console on the Service Provider side:

1. First, the backup from the tenant will need to be imported into the console by clicking the **Import Backup** button on the **Home** tab.

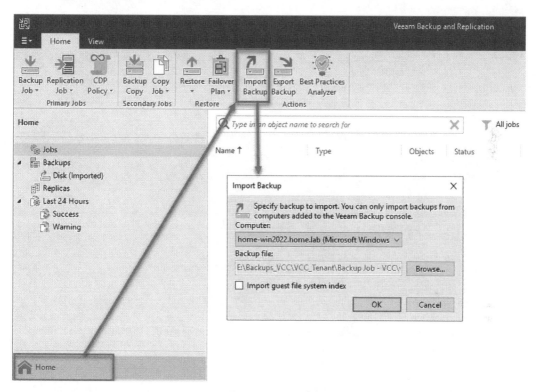

Figure 8.29 – Import Backup screen

2. Select the computer (that is the repository server), and click the **Browse…** button to select the VBK/VIB file for import. Click **OK** when finished. The backup will import into the console, and a new section in the tree will appear: **Backups > Disk (Imported)**.

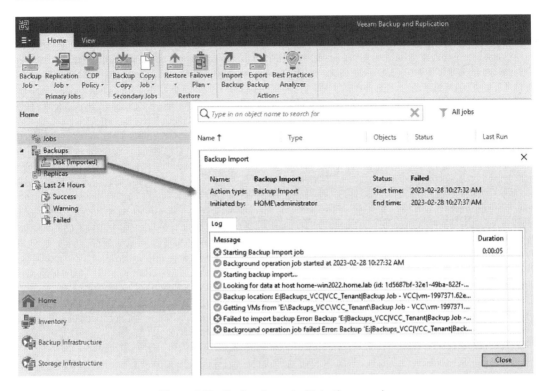

Figure 8.30 – Backup imported into the console

> **Note**
>
> The import backup failed as it was already imported, so the error for the **Backup Import** dialog can be safely ignored in this case.

3. Navigate to **Disk (Imported)**, expand the **Backup Job** listed, and select the VM to be recovered.

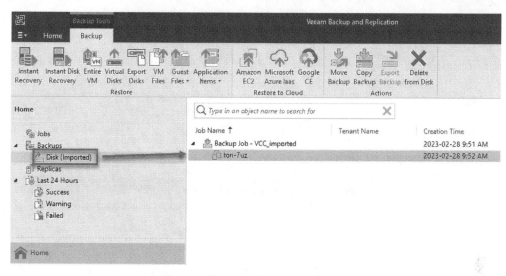

Figure 8.31 – VM selected for recovery

4. After selecting the VM to recover, you will notice that the toolbar options are now available. Select the **Instant Recovery** button from the toolbar to launch the **Instant Recovery to VMware vSphere** wizard.

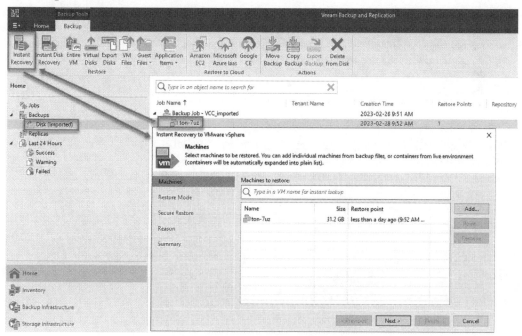

Figure 8.32 – Instant Recovery to VMware vSphere wizard

5. Select the restore point that you want to recover (in my test case, there is only one), and then click the **Next** button to proceed to the **Restore Mode** section.

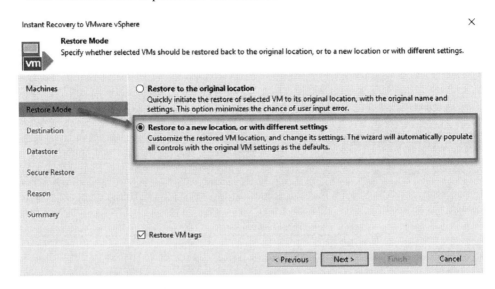

Figure 8.33 – Restore Mode screen

6. The Service Provider will need to select the **Restore to a new location, or with different settings** option since we are not doing the recovery on the tenant side. After selecting this option, click **Next** to move to the **Destination** screen.

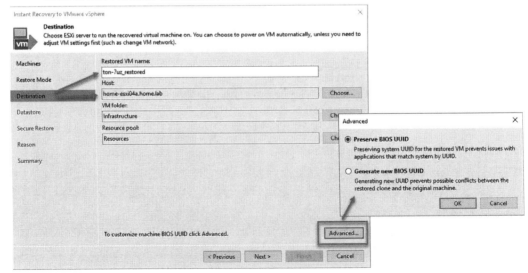

Figure 8.34 – Destination screen showing where to restore the VM

> **Note**
>
> Since I am testing this process in the same environment, I added `_restored` to the VM name to ensure no conflict with my current VM.

7. On the **Destination** screen, you will select options for **Host**, **VM folder**, and **Resource pool**, and you can use the **Advanced...** button to choose whether you keep the BIOS UUID or generate a new one. Since the restore is done from the provider side, you can leave the **Preserve BIOS UUID** option and click **Next** to proceed to the **Datastore** screen.

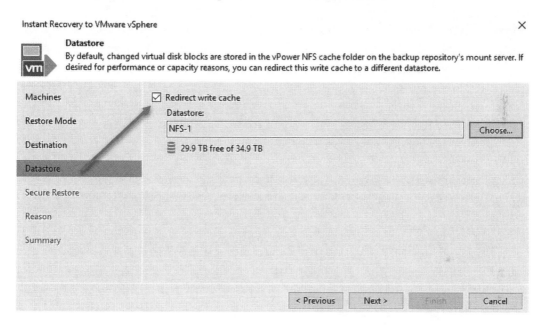

Figure 8.35 – Datastore screen for write cache redirection

8. When restoring a VM, it uses the vPower NFS cache folder on the repository where the mount service has been installed. If you prefer to have the write cache redirected to another datastore so as not to cause performance issues, select the checkbox and datastore using the **Choose...** button. Click **Next** to proceed to the **Secure Restore** screen.

> **Note**
>
> The write cache folder is where changes are written to while the VM runs and before the restore occurs. This allows you to target more performant storage.

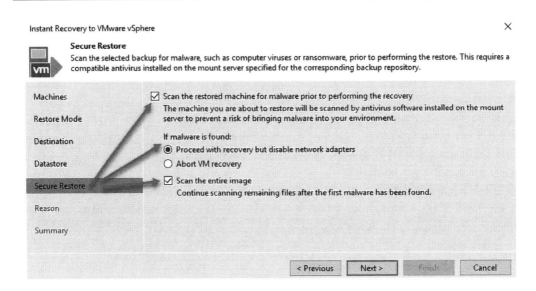

Figure 8.36 – Secure Restore screen for antivirus scanning

9. On the **Secure Restore** screen, you can turn on the VM's virus scanning during the restore process. Select the required options and click **Next** to move to the **Reason** screen.

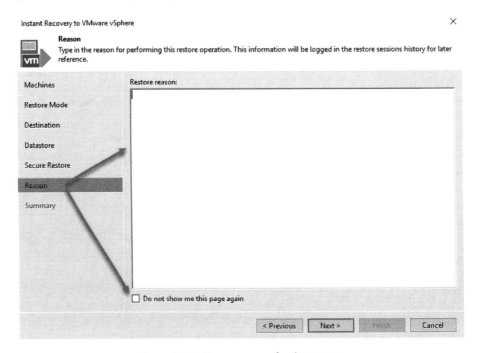

Figure 8.37 – Reason screen for the restore

10. After entering a restore reason, click **Next** to move to the final screen – **Summary** – to review and finish the instant VM recovery process.

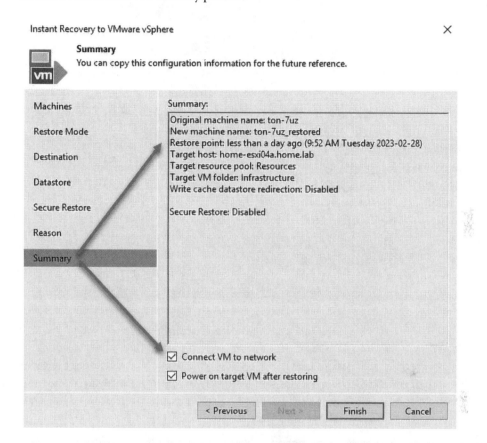

Figure 8.38 – Summary screen to review recovery options

11. On the **Summary** screen, you can check the restore information and turn on the **Connect VM to network** and **Power on target VM after restoring** options, depending on how you want to proceed. Once all options are set, click **Finish** to begin the recovery process.

12. You will see the **Restore Session** status window, and when done, you can now work to complete the restore from the **Instant Recovery** section, which is now in the tree on the console.

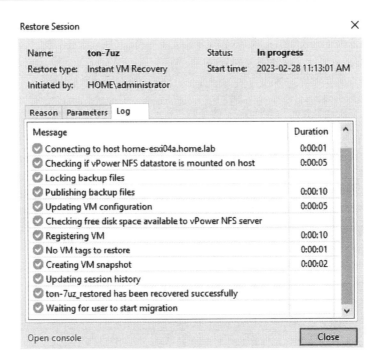

Figure 8.39 – Restore session dialog

13. When you click the **Instant Recovery** section in the console, you will notice the restore point is now mounted. There are options in the toolbar when you are ready to migrate the VM to production or stop the instant VM recovery. You can use the **Migrate to Production** button to complete the instant VM recovery or click **Stop Publishing** to cancel the task.

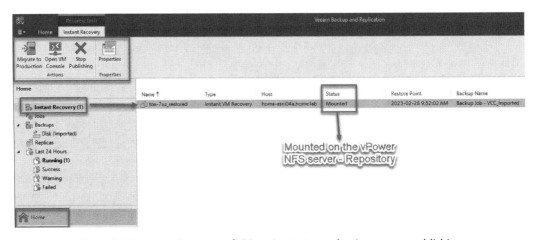

Figure 8.40 – Instant Recovery of VM – migrate to production or stop publishing

14. For this example, I will click **Stop Publishing** to cancel my restore. In the real world, a service provider might use the **Open VM Console** button to launch a console to log in to the VM, or use **Migrate to Production** to complete the restoration of the VM and allow the client access to it via VMware Cloud Director.

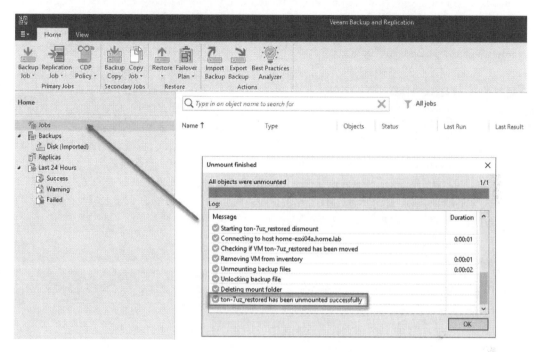

Figure 8.41 – Restore canceled and unmounted

That completes the process for a Service Provider to be able to make an instant VM recovery for a client backup and selected VMs. This process allows the service provider to provide both an added service for their client and even restore testing to ensure the backups are sound within the repository server to which clients are backing up.

Summary

In this chapter, we looked at the process of using CDP with Veeam Cloud Connect for a Service Provider using VMware Cloud Director. We reviewed the requirements and prerequisites for creating CDP policies and how to direct them to the VCC server.

We also discussed using CDP to protect vApps within VMware Cloud Director from one tenant vCD to another vCD.

Finally, you should understand how Service Providers can now provide an added service for their clients using the instant VM recovery feature. Hopefully, you will better understand how instant VM recovery works for Service Providers.

This chapter concludes the third edition of the *Mastering Veeam Backup & Replication v12* book, and I want to thank you for reading it. I hope this book's content will benefit you and help you configure your environment based on the topics covered, including many of the newest enhancements and features added to the Veeam products.

Further reading

- *CDP with Veeam Cloud Connect*: `https://helpcenter.veeam.com/docs/backup/cloud/cloud_connect_cdp.html?ver=120`

- *Backup Infrastructure for CDP*: `https://helpcenter.veeam.com/docs/backup/vsphere/cdp_infrastructure.html?ver=120`

- *CDP for VMware Cloud Director*: `https://helpcenter.veeam.com/docs/backup/vsphere/vcloud_director_cdp.html?ver=120`

- *Continuous Data Protection (CDP)*: `https://helpcenter.veeam.com/docs/backup/vsphere/cdp_replication.html?ver=120`

- Best Practice for Instant VM Recovery: `https://bp.veeam.com/vbr/Support/S_Vmware/instant_vm_recovery.html`

Index

A

access control list (ACL) 149
Amazon Simple Storage Service (S3) 132
Application drive 4
Archive extents 24
Archive Tier 26
auto logoff feature
  discovering 117-119

B

backup copy job
  configuring, with GFS retention to
    immutable object storage 133-139
backup data direct
  sending, to Object Storage with SOBR 64-66
backup file placement
  reference link 27
Backup from Storage Snapshots 18

C

Capacity extents 24
Capacity Tier 26-28
  options 31

reference link 29
  using, reasons 28
Catalog drive 4
cloud helper appliance 165-171
Configuration Backups 14
Continuous Data Protection (CDP) 18
  Backup Server 174
  CDP proxy 174
  discovering, to vCD in Veeam
    Cloud Connect 173-185
  exploring, with vCD to vCD 186-194
  I/O Filters 174
  Source and Target Hosts 174
Continuous Data Protection (CDP) role 58
CREATEDB role 49
cyclic redundancy check (CRC) 163

D

data
  exporting 72
Default Backup Repository 14
Direct NFS 18
Direct Storage Access mode 18
direct-to-object storage 122, 146
disaster recovery (DR) site 133

E

Enterprise Manager (EM) 50
Extents
    types 65

F

File Backup Proxy 14
formats, for storing files on repository server
    per machine or split machine 52
    single storage 51
    true per machine 53

G

GFS backups
    immutability, used for sending to
        object storage 132, 133
group-managed service accounts
        (gMSA) 107
    benefits 113-116

H

health check utility 163-165
Hot-Add Mode 18

I

immutable repositories
    NAS backup with 152-155
Instant VM Recovery
    investigating, within Veeam
        Cloud Connect 194-203
integration with storage systems
    reference link 18

Internet Small Computer System
        Interface (iSCSI) 97
ISO file 5

L

limitation of concurrent tasks
    reference link 21
limitations for Scale-Out
        Backup Repositories
    reference link 26
Linux 117
    using, for tape server 84-90
Linux Backup Repositories 24
Linux hardened repository option
    in repository wizard 54-57
Linux proxy
    roles 57-60
long-term storage (LTR) 97

M

Microsoft Azure storage
    adding 141, 142
multi-factor authentication (MFA) 107-112
    additional settings 112, 113

N

network-attached storage (NAS)
        backup 143-146
    archive copy mode 146-152
    direct-to-object storage 146-152
    using, to improved LTO9 support 96-98
    using, to tape 96-98
    with immutable repositories 152-155
network file system (NFS) backup 143
    publishing, as SMB share 155-162

Network mode 18
No Per-VM Selection 23

O

Object Storage 24, 63, 121
    backing up, to tape 90-96
Object Storage with SOBR
    backup data direct, sending to 64-66
    benefits 65
OS drive 4

P

Performance extents 24
Performance Tier 26
    reference link 27
per-VM backup chains 51-54
Per-VM Backup Files 22
physical tape
    versus virtual tape 97
placement policies, types
    data locality 27
    performance 27
PostgreSQL server 48, 49
    installation 50
Proxy Servers 17
    configuring 17-21
    operating system 19
    optimizing 17-21
    proxy placement 19
    proxy sizing 19
    tasks 18

Q

Quadstor Virtual Tape Library (VTL) 84

R

Recovery Time Objective (RTO) 173
Remote Desktop (RDP) 117
Repository Server 14
    task limit 23
    setting up 21-24
Repository Servers, setting up
    ReFS/XFS 21
    sizing 21
Resource Scheduler (RTS) 73

S

Scale-Out Backup Repository (SOBR)
        15, 24, 25, 30, 51, 63, 90
    Archive Tier 26
    Capacity Tier 26, 31, 32
    Enterprise 25
    Enterprise Plus & VUL (Veeam
        Universal License) 25
    jobs/tasks 25
    limitations 25, 26
    managing 33
    Performance Tier 26, 30, 31
    reference link 32, 33
    VeeaMover 33
scale-out repository 64
    benefits 65
Sealed Mode 33
Secure Shell (SSH) 107
Server Message Block (SMB) share 143
    NFS backup, publishing as 155-162
Service-Level Agreement (SLA) 97, 173
service principal name (SPN) 113
Shared Folder 24
SOBR backup job 132
SOBR Rebalance 33

backups, exporting 76-81

feature 72-75

limitations 75

placement policies 72

using 72

SQL Server, moving to PostgreSQL server

benefits 50

standalone managed service account (sMSA) 113

standard repository 64

standard repository backup job 131

super user do (SUDO) 107

T

tape

NAS backup, using 96-98

object storage 84

object storage, backing up to 90-96

tape server

Linux, using 84-90

version update 84

third-party integrations

discovering, within console for Azure and Wasabi 139

transport mode 18

V

Veeam Alliance Technical Programs

reference link 32

Veeam Backup & Replication (VBR) 63

reference link 66

upgrading, to v12 34-44

Veeam Backup & Replication (VBR) v12 107, 143

enhancements 98-104

installing 4-17

Proxy Servers 17

Veeam backup repository design

reference link 21

Veeam Certified Service Provider (VCSP) 175

Veeam Cloud Connect

CDP, discovering to vCD 173-185

Instant VM Recovery, investigating within 194-203

Veeam Data Mover 18

Veeam Enterprise Manager 34

Veeam installation

best practices 4

optimizations 4

Veeam Installer Service 18

VeeaMover 33, 66

benefits 66

exploring 66

use cases 66-72

Veeam VMware vSphere backup proxy

reference link 17

Virtual Appliance mode 18

virtual tape library (VTL) 97

versus physical tape 97

VMware Backup Proxy 14

reference link 17

VMware vStorage APIs for Data Protection (VADP) 19

W

Wasabi-3 130, 131

Wasabi-4/Wasabi-5 130, 131

Wasabi Object storage

adding 122-130, 140

Windows Backup Repositories 24

Packtpub.com

Subscribe to our online digital library for full access to over 7,000 books and videos, as well as industry leading tools to help you plan your personal development and advance your career. For more information, please visit our website.

Why subscribe?

- Spend less time learning and more time coding with practical eBooks and Videos from over 4,000 industry professionals

- Improve your learning with Skill Plans built especially for you

- Get a free eBook or video every month

- Fully searchable for easy access to vital information

- Copy and paste, print, and bookmark content

Did you know that Packt offers eBook versions of every book published, with PDF and ePub files available? You can upgrade to the eBook version at packtpub.com and as a print book customer, you are entitled to a discount on the eBook copy. Get in touch with us at customercare@packtpub.com for more details.

At www.packtpub.com, you can also read a collection of free technical articles, sign up for a range of free newsletters, and receive exclusive discounts and offers on Packt books and eBooks.

Other Books You May Enjoy

If you enjoyed this book, you may be interested in these other books by Packt:

The Vulnerability Researcher's Handbook

Benjamin Strout

ISBN: 978-1-80323-887-6

- Find out what zero-day vulnerabilities are and why it's so important to disclose and publish them

- Learn how vulnerabilities get discovered and published to vulnerability scanning tools

- Explore successful strategies for starting and executing vulnerability research

- Discover ways to disclose zero-day vulnerabilities responsibly

- Populate zero-day security findings into the CVE databases

- Navigate and resolve conflicts with hostile vendors

- Publish findings and receive professional credit for your work

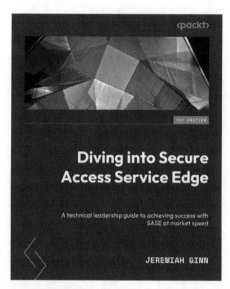

Diving into Secure Access Service Edge

Jeremiah Ginn

ISBN: 978-1-80324-217-0

- Develop a comprehensive understanding of SASE from a market and technical perspective
- Understand SASE services and components included in SASE solutions
- Move logically from prescriptive design to policy-based design and orchestration
- Understand standard SASE use cases and how to integrate future components
- Convert from a legacy network design model to a secure DevOps model for future projects
- Use a functional design overlay to eliminate inter-service competition for the control plane of the SASE service

Packt is searching for authors like you

If you're interested in becoming an author for Packt, please visit `authors.packtpub.com` and apply today. We have worked with thousands of developers and tech professionals, just like you, to help them share their insight with the global tech community. You can make a general application, apply for a specific hot topic that we are recruiting an author for, or submit your own idea.

Share Your Thoughts

Now you've finished *Mastering Veeam Backup & Replication*, we'd love to hear your thoughts! Scan the QR code below to go straight to the Amazon review page for this book and share your feedback or leave a review on the site that you purchased it from.

`https://packt.link/r/1837630097`

Your review is important to us and the tech community and will help us make sure we're delivering excellent quality content.

Download a free PDF copy of this book

Thanks for purchasing this book!

Do you like to read on the go but are unable to carry your print books everywhere?

Is your eBook purchase not compatible with the device of your choice?

Don't worry, now with every Packt book you get a DRM-free PDF version of that book at no cost.

Read anywhere, any place, on any device. Search, copy, and paste code from your favorite technical books directly into your application.

The perks don't stop there, you can get exclusive access to discounts, newsletters, and great free content in your inbox daily

Follow these simple steps to get the benefits:

1. Scan the QR code or visit the link below

https://packt.link/free-ebook/9781837630097

2. Submit your proof of purchase
3. That's it! We'll send your free PDF and other benefits to your email directly

Made in the USA
Middletown, DE
03 November 2023